W9-ANG-324

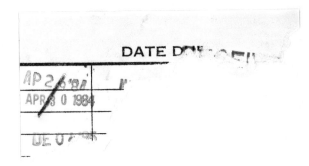

Costumes and Settings for Shakespeare's Plays

John T. Williams

Drawings by Jack Cassin-Scott

Barnes & Noble Books
Totswa, New Jersey

To Sarah — my belated homework.

Printed in Great Britain

First published in the USA 1982 by
Barnes & Noble Books
81 Adams Drive
Totswa, New Jersey, 07512

ISBN 0-389-20322-X

Contents

Text references and quotations from The Players Edition of *William Shakespeare, the Complete Works*, edited with an introduction and glossary by Peter Alexander, published by Collins.

PART ONE

What this book is about

There are nine and sixty ways of constructing tribal lays. And-every-single-one-of-them-is-right! (Kipling: 'In the Neolithic Age'). Successful and valid ways of producing Shakespeare seem to be almost equally numerous: historically accurate reproductions of sixteenth-century theatre; equally accurate reproductions of the period in which a given play is set; productions in nineteenth-century décor, in modern dress, in settings and costumes deliberately remote from any known period, in track-suits and in pvc — all of these have appeared in recent years, and every type has pleased at least some audiences and illuminated some aspect of Shakespeare's work. Faced with this variety, a producer may well feel bewildered. He may find it equally difficult to choose a style, and, having chosen it, to carry it out. I hope this book will help to solve both these problems, and that it will be useful to all involved in a Shakespearian production.

The first part gives a brief historical sketch of Shakespeare in the theatre from his own time to the present day. This will show how his dramatic genius has triumphed in every theatrical convention for over four centuries. It will show too how initmately his genius was related to his first-hand, practical knowledge of his own theatre. This close connection explains many characteristic features of Shakespearian drama, and thereby helps a modern producer to interpret them.

Examination of how Shakespeare's plays have been produced leads naturally to a consideration of basic principles of Shakespearian production. Is there one ideal style for all his plays? Is there an ideal style for each? How far should choice be influenced by the essential qualities of the play itself? How far by the skills of a given group of performers? How far by the material conditions of production, especially by that most material condition, the amount of money available? These and other relevant problems are discussed, and ideas are suggested which should contribute to a satisfactory solution. I should like to emphasize the words 'suggest' and 'contribute'. Anyone who is fit to produce even the humblest one-act piece must have his or her own ideas and tastes. It would be quite wrong for even the most eminent Shakespearian scholar or the most experienced Shakespearian producer to prescribe dogmatically how somebody else should produce one of Shakespeare's plays. Guidance, on the other hand, can be valuable, both in reaching the total concept of a production and in the details of its execution.

Therefore the second part applies the basic principles of the book to ten plays chosen from the Shakespearian canon. The ten have been chosen to illustrate a wide range of his work and a correspondingly wide range of production styles.

At the back of the book, there is a glossary of technical terms, to avoid repeated explanations.

Shakespeare in the theatre: a brief historical sketch

The aims of this chapter are to show the enormous variety of production styles which have been used in the last four centuries, and thus the variety open to a modern producer, and also to emphasize how powerfully circumstances influence production. The variety is, of course, potentially much greater than the number of actual historical styles, since these may be combined in different ways or suggest styles totally new. The power of circumstances reminds us that no play is performed in a vacuum: from the tone of the whole social environment, through current theatrical conventions, to the size and shape of the auditorium and the physique of the performers, the production is sometimes inspired by particular opportunities and sometimes fettered by particular restrictions. When a producer feels frustrated, as every producer does at times, he may console himself by remembering that Shakespeare must often have felt the same. He too had to work with the inevitable imperfections of his actors, with the limitations of particular theatrical conditions — and under the eye of a politically suspicious censorship. While only an outstanding producer can hope for a touch of the genius by which Shakespeare transcended these limitations, an ordinarily intelligent one may develop the technical skill which can turn many of these restrictions into opportunities for theatrical triumphs.

Thus, though the history of Shakespeare in the theatre has an intrinsic interest for anyone concerned in producing him, our emphasis will be on those aspects that have a practical value to the contemporary producer.

Shakespeare in his own time

In his own lifetime, Shakespeare's plays were performed, for the most part, in three different kinds of setting: the public theatres; the so-called private theatres; and the halls of great houses, colleges and the Inns of Court. Each of these had its own characteristics, but we must not exaggerate the differences: many of his plays were performed in all these settings. Nevertheless, both the material conditions of stage and auditorium, and the kind of audience to be expected, clearly influenced what he wrote, and perhaps what he avoided writing.

The public theatres We shall begin with these, for it is here that Shakespeare made his name; here that most of his plays probably had their first performances, and it was their appeal both to connoisseur and populace, to 'the judicious' and 'the many-headed' alike, that was the unique glory of the Elizabethan and Jacobean theatre.

Though lack of evidence leaves much uncertain, there seems wide agreement about some basic features of the sixteenth-century public theatres.

There was a platform stage projecting into a yard, so that spectators were on three sides of it. At the back, was a curtained, or possibly doored, recess (the Inner Stage); above that, a small upper stage and perhaps a gallery. Below the stage, was the 'cellarage', into which, for example, the cauldron in *Macbeth* could disappear. Above was a roof, often with stars or the Signs of the Zodiac painted on it. For a few pence, spectators could simply stand in the yard; hence their name, the ground-lings'. For a higher price, one could sit under cover in the galleries that surrounded the yard. A few privileged persons, usually courtiers who prided themselves on being patrons of the theatre, occasionally sat on the stage itself. Even the most enthusiastic admirer of Elizabethan theatre might have doubts about reviving that particular custom!

This plan, which had many variations, was derived from the stages set up by travelling actors in inn-yards. (The typical sixteenth-century inn took the form of a hollow square round a yard, and the upper rooms were entered from galleries running round the inner or courtyard side of the building.)

The first permanent theatre in England was built in 1576, only twelve years after Shakespeare was born. Named simply The Theatre, it was set up by John Burbage, father of the great Richard Burbage, who played most of Shakespeare's leading roles for the first time. The Theatre soon moved from its original site to the South Bank of the Thames, where it was outside the jurisdiction of the usually hostile City authorities and yet near to its potential audiences. Hence other theatres were soon built there; the most famous, and the one that most concerns us was the Globe, the home of Shakespeare's own company, the Lord Chamberlain's Men, afterwards the King's Men.

Two characteristics of Shakespeare's theatre strike us at once: the close contact between actor and audience, and the comparative absence of scenery. Three effects they had in common: the speed with which scene succeeded scene; the author's ability to rely on his audience's responding to language that was often complex and subtle; and the need to use dialogue to indicate place when this was necessary. We can also see why

every scene begins with an entrance and ends with an exit. There was no curtain, so there was no possibility of characters being 'discovered' on the main stage. For the same reason, they could not be left in an effective tableau. They had to make an exit. One of the most obvious examples of Shakespeare's genius in turning a material necessity into an artistic triumph is the ending of many of his tragedies. Think of the ending of *Hamlet*, when Fortinbras gives the command:

> Let four captains
> Bear Hamlet like a soldier from the stage;
> For he was likely, had he been put on,
> To have prov'd most royal; . . .
> Go, bid the soldiers shoot.

Here the end is not only a magnificent piece of theatre, but a powerful reminder of the Hamlet that might have been.

The end of *Coriolanus* is so similar and so profoundly different. Again, a hero, but of a totally different sort, had died violently. Here his epitaph is spoken, not by a neutral admirer, but by the very man who has organized his death.

> *Aufidius*   My rage is gone,
> And I am struck with sorrow. Take him up.
> Help three of the chiefest soldiers; I'll be one.
> Beat thou the drum, that it speak mournfully
> Trail your steel pikes. Though in this city he
> Hath widowed and unchilded many a one
> Yet he shall have a noble memory.
> Assist.

In both scenes, a solemn military procession marks the end of a tragic hero. Both incorporate specific directions as to sound effects. But Fortinbras emphasizes the lost potentialities of Hamlet; Aufidius reminds us of the actual prowess of Coriolanus, and that he died an exile in the city of his enemies. Each sums up, at this final moment, the special tragedy of the hero: the destruction of Hamlet and all his promise by a task beyond his scope; the destruction of Coriolanus by 'His own impatience'. Each too exploits the special effectiveness of a tribute from an alien or hostile source. What a superb combination of dramatic effects arising from the material need to get a crowd of actors off the stage!

bareness of the stage had definite
\akespeare and his public inherited
.al dramatic tradition which allowed the
_ge to represent anything from its actual
dimensions to a distance of many miles. In *The
Winter's Tale*, mere exits and entrances are enough
to take us from Sicily to Bohemia and back again.
Spectators were so accustomed to a non-naturalistic
convention, that Shakespeare could appeal openly
to their imaginations, as he does repeatedly in
the Chorus speeches in *Henry V*. He was confident
enough to remind them, sometimes at moments of
great emotional tension, that they were watching a
play. Immediately after the assassination of Caesar,
he makes Cassius say:

> How many ages hence
> Shall this our lofty scene he acted over
> In states unborn and accents yet unknown!

Brutus's answer drives the message home:

> How many times shall Caesar bleed in sport.

When he is building up to one of the greatest of all
his tragic closes, Cleopatra's royal marriage with
death, he makes Cleopatra remind the audience
that this magically attractive woman was being
played by a boy:

> I shall see
> Some squeaking Cleopatra boy my greatness
> I' th' posture of a whore.

It is, of course, important to remember that
Shakespeare's stage was not just a bare platform.
There is convincing evidence that it contained
trapdoors, which might be used for the cauldrons
and apparitions in *Macbeth*. [1] There was machinery
for flying, setting and striking furniture. [2] A *small*
group of characters could be discovered in the
Inner Stage, as Ferdinand and Miranda are discovered playing chess in *The Tempest*. The Upper
Stage allowed for a different level — often a visual
advantage in itself — and satisfied the needs of the
Balcony scene in *Romeo and Juliet* and the many
parleys between besiegers and besieged in the
Histories.

Many recent productions have been as bare
scenically as those of the sixteenth century. In one
respect, they have been much barer, for the older
theatres often made up in magnificence of costume
for what they lacked in scenery. Here we have a
valuable source of information in the diaries and
papers of Philip Henslowe, who owned several
theatres in Shakespeare's London. Henslowe
was primarily a business man; consequently, his
records are full of financial details of contracts
with dramatists and builders, but often tantalizingly
short of the information we should now prize
most. We have, for example, the contract for the
building of the Fortune Theatre, which tells us the
materials and some of the dimensions, but omits
details which would settle many long-standing
arguments. He did, however, record a good deal
about costumes, no doubt because they were a
valuable financial asset.

The impression he gives of rich and colourful
costumes is confirmed by several other witnesses,
including Sir Henry Wotton, courtier and poet,
who was present at the disastrous performance of
Henry VIII at the Globe in 1613, when the
thatched roof caught fire and the theatre was
destroyed. He comments on the 'many extraord-
inary circumstances of pomp and majesty . . . the
knights of the Order (of the Garter) with their
Georges and Garters, the Guards with their coats'.
It is clear that here, at least, care has been taken
to get the details right, though they can hardly
have had such august aid as a more recent Henry
VIII — Anthony Eustrel — when the late King
George VI asked if he might adjust the actor's
Garter, saying, 'I am rather an expert on these
things'.

Careful attention to costume was natural in
Shakespeare's time, when the cost of fashionable
clothes, with their rich materials lavishly decorated with jewels, was proportionately higher than
ever before or since in England. Magnificent
though they were, there was little attempt at the
sort of historical accuracy that the Romantic
movement brought to stage costume in the early
nineteenth century. Shakespeare's plays are
notoriously full of anachronisms, such as
Cleopatra's 'Cut my lace, Charmian', which
indicates she was wearing the laced bodice of the
author's time rather than any approximation to
the dress of an Egyptian lady in the first century
BC. Both words and contemporary illustrations

show that Shakespeare's Roman plays were originally performed in the mixture of contemporary and classical that we see in many Renaissance paintings of classical subjects.

Another striking characteristic of the public theatres was their dependence on daylight. When one thinks how many effects, subtle and spectacular, are now created by lighting, one realizes the problems that natural lighting must have posed. Even today, however, many successful performances have been given out of doors; for example, the long series of Shakesperian productions in the open-air theatre in Regent's Park. Obviously, some plays are much better suited to such conditions. *A Midsummer Night's Dream* has often been at its most magical on a summer evening. The Arcadian atmosphere of *As You Like It* has also worked powerfully, except when the wind has blown too wintrily and unkindly for the audience, not to mention the actors.

Like the absence of scenery, the absence of lighting was often supplied by the words: 'Look where the dawn in russet mantle clad' (*Hamlet*) and 'Light thickens, and the crow/ Makes wing to th' rooky wood' (*Macbeth*) are two opposite examples. Indeed, one of the temptations of a modern producer equipped with a full battery of sound effects is to swamp instead of supplementing the text. One has seen the storm in *Lear* full of magnificent but overwhelming effects which have drowned the words that create the storm far more powerfully than the finest stage thunder and lightning can possibly do.

One may sum up then by saying that the public theatre of Shakespeare's time was a superbly flexible and powerful instrument for a great dramatist. It lacked some kinds of equipment we take for granted, but it was very far from being primitive. It had absorbed the traditions of medieval stagecraft and added the Renaissance appreciation of trained speaking and gesture. Above all, it had close contact with a varied audience used to listening to language that was often elaborate and difficult. No doubt, many of them were what Hamlet called 'barren spectators', whose appreciation did not extend beyond crude melodrama and bawdry; but these are, after all, deep and vital elements in human feeling. And if

many had not also been able to appreciate subtle characterization and superb poetry, Shakespeare could not have been a successful man of the theatre as well as the greatest dramatist the world has yet known.

Private theatres and halls Just as the public theatres developed from occasional performances in inn yards, so the private theatres developed from performances in the halls of colleges, Inns of Court, great houses, and the greatest of all houses, the royal palaces. The name 'private' is misleading, as the public were admitted, but prices were higher, so the audiences tended to be higher in rank and more sophisticated in taste. In addition to the influence this might have on text and presentation, there were important material differences. The actors were probably more separated from their audience, though there is evidence of performance in the round. Artificial lighting was essential, and more elaborate stage effects were practicable. Another vital difference was the roof which gave complete shelter from the weather. One supposes this must have led to a more restrained style of acting than that of the public theatres, where a very powerful voice projection must have been needed to fill an open auditorium and overcome the intrusive sounds of the outer world – another example of the close relation of environment with acting.

Originally the private theatres were used by the temporarily popular Boys of St Paul's and the Children of the Chapel Royal – the 'little eyases' (young hawks) referred to in *Hamlet* (II.2. 336) who performed at the Blackfriars Theatre; but after their brief success, the King's Men took over in 1608, and used it during the winters when the weather would have prevented performances at the open Globe.

Court performances were probably an even greater influence on Shakespeare. The records of the Treasurer of the Chamber and the Master of the Revels [3] (the officials responsible for Court entertainments) are an invaluable source for the theatrical history of the time. They confirm that Shakespeare's plays did indeed 'take Eliza and our James', as Ben Jonson [4] wrote in his prefatory poem to the First Folio.

Court performance posed special problems as well as giving special advantages. The author had to consider the tastes and susceptibilities of the monarch. *Macbeth* is a striking example of this. Whether the version we have is Shakespeare's original or one shortened for Court use, the favourable presentation of Banquo, King James's legendary ancestor, the otherwise rather surprising emphasis on King Edward the Confessor's power of healing scrofula (a power which James claimed to inherit) and the even greater emphasis on witchcraft, on which James himself had written a book — all show how Shakespeare could write to please a special audience, even a special auditor. They also show how he could transcend this need.

Again, whether or not one is convinced by Dr Hotson's [5] account of 'The First Night of *Twelfth Night*', the suggestion that the satirical portrait of Malvolio was a recognizable mockery of Sir William Knollys (pronounced and sometimes written Knowles) the Comptroller of the Queen's Household, who had just made a conspicuous fool of himself by his pursuit of Mary (Mal) Fitton, an attractive Maid of Honour, young enough to be his daughter, makes us aware of the potential relationship of dramatist to audience. Similarly, Dr Hotson's picture of the actual production reminds us of the choice open to Shakespeare and his contemporaries. Theatre in the round and mansions or pavilions were inherited from the medieval stage; the impenetrability of disguise and its special application to a boy actor playing a girl disguising 'herself' as a young man were conventions of Shakespeare's own day.

Troilus and Cressida is perhaps the best example of how an audience other than the Court could affect a play. There is strong probability that it was written for some festivity at one of the Inns of Court. The combination of debate and legal terminology with bawdry and a cynical attitude both to love and to traditional authority would please what was virtually an undergraduate audience with special knowledge of the law. This may explain why it has been one of Shakespeare's least popular plays. There is hardly any character with which the average audience would identify — 'All incontinent varlets' as its own bitter Thersites says — and perhaps this too was specially appropriate to an audience including so many budding lawyers, whose future would bind them often to argue their client's case while remaining personally detached.

While the Court was a valuable patron, it could also restrain and threaten. Many readers and spectators must have wondered why Shakespeare's characters often swear by 'Jove' in non-classical plays, or say 'Heaven' when 'God' would seem more natural and metrically apt. The explanation often lies in the Act of Abuses (1606) which forbade stage plays to use the names of God, Christ Jesus and the Trinity. This helps to explain why Shakespeare's language is more guarded in his later plays. When early plays appear to obey the Act, some scholars interpret this as a sign of later revision, but the Act was applied so inconsistently that it seems dangerous to base much on such evidence.

All plays, like other publications, were subject to censorship. This particularly affected the Histories, where parallels might be drawn between past and present. To make the dramatist's position still more precarious, a parallel safe at the time of writing might become dangerous through a change in the political situation. Thus Shakespeare's flattering comparison between the triumph of Henry V (Prologue to Act V) and hopes for the triumph of Essex over the Irish rebels was safe, perhaps even profitable, as long as Essex was the Queen's favourite, but much less so when he returned from Ireland to disgrace, and positively dangerous after Essex's abortive *coup d'état*. The danger was intensified by the fact that Essex's supporters arranged a performance of *Richard II* by the Lord Chamberlain's Men the day before the rising. Even earlier, the authorities had insisted that Richard's abdication scene must be cut. Knowing how long and successfully Elizabeth I reigned, we find it hard to imagine how precarious her position often seemed to her enemies, to her friends; above all, to herself. Hence she was extremely sensitive to any suggestion that a monarch could be lawfully deposed, or forced, even persuaded, to abdicate. Nor was she sensitive only to such suggestions in general: at the time of the Essex rising, she exclaimed, 'Know ye not that I am Richard II?' All things considered, the company was lucky to escape punishment or at least the Queen's lasting displeasure.

Royal susceptibilities, censorship and politically sensitive situations were not the only conditions which Shakespeare had to accept. He had to work with the conventions of his theatre, one of which, the impenetrability of disguise, is closely connected with the last characteristic to be considered in this chapter: the nature of the companies with which he worked.

It is often hard for a modern spectator of *Twelfth Night* or *As You Like It* to accept that anyone could possibly mistake a sometimes voluptuously bosomed Viola or Rosalind for a young man. Some cannot swallow it at all. Some do not really expect Shakespeare to make sense. Some achieve partial acceptance by remembering the pantomime tradition of the Principal Boy. And some, of course, do know the historical fact that in Shakespeare's time there were no actresses, and that boys played the female roles. This was the most obvious difference between his companies and nearly all those in England for the last three centuries. It explains why there are so few female characters in the plays of that era: there must have been few boys who had all the dramatic skills to play Lady Macbeth or Cleopatra, and by the time they had acquired the skills, growth or a broken voice would soon destroy their acceptability. No dramatist could then rely on a glamorous sex-symbol to charm his audience. The words, spoken with highest degree of professional skill, had to carry the major burden.

These all-male companies were usually at least semi-permanent, and organized on a profit-sharing basis so far as their senior members were concerned. For most of his working life, Shakespeare was an active member of, and for years a shareholder in, his company. Apart from commonsense probability, there is internal evidence of how working closely with a known group of actors affected his writings. Many scholars agree, for example, that the change from the servant clowns of his early plays to the subtler, more poetic court fools like Feste and the Fool in *Lear* was due partly to Kempe's replacement by Armin as the company's principal comic actor, as well as to Shakespeare's development. Bernard Shaw, another dramatist who took an active part in the production of his plays, commented that Shakespeare's progress from *Richard III* to *Hamlet* must have had some connection with Richard Burbage's development as an actor. Certainly every producer must ask himself whether the play he wants to produce is within the scope of his company.

Names like the Lord Chamberlain's Men, the King's Men, Lord Strange's Men and other names of sixteenth and seventeenth-century companies remind us of the precarious legal position of actors. As such, they were classed as rogues and vagabonds, and subject to harsh penalties. They could escape this status only by becoming officially the liveried servants of a nobleman. In return for his patronage and protection, they were bound to perform for him on such occasions as Christmas, family birthdays and weddings. For the rest of the year, they were free for the public. Shakespeare was particularly fortunate in belonging to a company patronised first by a major Court official, and then by the King himself.

I hope this account of Shakespeare's theatre has shown how intimately his plays were linked with their environment, material and cultural; and how he both accepted and transcended the limitations this environment imposed. We shall now see how his work survived mutilation and then idolatry, and triumphed in the most varied conditions. I hope, too, that this section and those that follow will answer specific questions and supply a variety of ideas.

From Shakespeare's death to the Commonwealth

Between Shakespeare's death (1616) and the Commonwealth (1649-1660) the trends already established in his later years continued, especially the greater emphasis on spectacle.

In purely Shakespearian history, the most important event was the publication of his collected plays in 1623. This collection, known as the First Folio, edited by Heminge and Condell, two of his former partners in the King's Men, show that Shakespeare had already achieved near classic status; folio volumes were still mainly reserved for serious scholarly works. The plays were introduced by two dedications in prose by the editors, and by several poems in praise of Shakespeare; Ben Jonson's including the famous and prophetic 'He was not for an age, but for all time!' Even allowing for the polite conventions of such writing — and for what we know of Jonson's more critical comments elsewhere — the evidence of Shakespeare's accepted greatness is impressive. More valuable practically, the First Folio gives fairly good texts of 36 of the 37 plays usually attributed to Shakespeare, *Pericles* being omitted. For 18, this is the earliest text we have. The other 18 allow comparison with the earlier Quarto publication of individual plays.

From the Restoration to Romanticism

The Commonwealth marks a great divide in the history of the English theatre. For 11 years, theatres were closed. When they reopened at the Restoration of Charles II in 1660, they were radically different. Actresses took over the female roles. London theatres were a more elaborate and luxurious version of the early private theatres. Audiences consisted mainly of courtiers and court hangers-on. The leading contemporary dramatists belonged at least to the fringes of the Court. Critical taste was founded on French neo-classicism. Though the Court had been a powerful influence in Shakespeare's life, he had also appealed to a much wider, more popular audience. Now the Court was totally dominant.

How did Shakespeare fare in this very different world? The stricter neo-classical critics attacked him for mingling comedy with tragedy, for scenes of low buffoonery, or excessive violence, and for violating the Unities. On the other hand, Dryden, the dominant literary figure of the age, and himself one of its most successful dramatists, admired him and wrote some of the best early criticism of his work. Several of his plays were performed, but in adaptations to conform to changes in taste. *Romeo and Juliet* and *Lear* were given happy endings. Davenant added singing and dancing to *Macbeth*. *The Tempest* and *A Midsummer Night's Dream* were turned into operas, the latter with music by Purcell. These, and other similarly free adaptations, flourished well beyond the Resto-

ration, which lasted theatrically till the beginning of the eighteenth century.

Just as the neo-classical taste had only a partial and temporary dominance in England, so the Restoration playhouse compromised between the close audience-performer contact of Shakespeare's day and the rigid demarcation of the seventeenth century French theatre. The old platform stage shrank to an apron, but the apron kept performers close to the audience, especially as it seems much of the action took place on it. The new proscenium arch also had a double effect. By framing the main stage like a picture it separated whatever was on it from the audience, but it also contained the entrances to the apron. Scenery consisted mainly of painted backcloths, and this combined with use of the apron to place the action in front of rather than in the set. The backcloths themselves consisted of a range of typical scenes that could be used for many different plays.

In the eighteenth century, the use of flats developed, while the apron disappeared from London theatres to make room for more seats. The performers were now completely framed by the proscenium arch, and further separated from the audience by an orchestra pit, a pattern which became standard for English theatres until the middle of this century.

Costumes long followed the traditions of Shakespeare's time by combining contemporary dress with often rather arbitrary exceptions. Just as an early seventeenth century illustration shows Cleopatra in the dress of a Jacobean court lady talking to, presumably, Antony wearing recognizable Roman armour, so an illustration in Rowe's Shakespeare's (1709) shows Gertrude and Hamlet in eighteenth century dress, while the Ghost is 'clad in complete steel'. The great Garrick continued to wear eighteenth-century dress for the major Shakespearian roles, though he did move, a little and tentatively, towards restoring Shakespeare's text, or at least his plots. Later in the century, Macklin and Kemble put Macbeth into Highland costume, but Kemble still played Lear, Othello and Richard III in contemporary dress. A mixture of contemporary and Roman remained common in eighteenth-century productions with a classical setting. Tragic actresses usually wore the hooped skirts and hairstyles of their own time with a voluminous veil and a 'forest of feathers'. Actors paid more attention to history, normally in the form of a tunic with labels. Kemble's sister, Sarah Siddons, the greatest tragic actress of her time, was also the first to discard the hoops and the massive headgear, and probably influenced her brother in his attempts at authentic Roman costumes and settings in *Coriolanus*. Forster criticized the crowding together of architectural features from different parts of Rome, but admitted the ideal grandeur of the total effect, and Coriolanus was generally considered Kemble's masterpiece.

Romanticism: antiquarian accuracy and the restoration of Shakespeare's text

Theatrical history, like other history, refuses to fit into a neat pattern. Old styles survive in the midst of new; revolution hardens into a fresh orthodoxy, to be challenged by a newer revolution; and only to very limited extent may we label a style with the name of its century. Thus the restoration of Shakespeare unadapted was hardly complete till 1850, and even then he was often severely cut; partly to conciliate Victorian standards of decency, but much more to give time for elaborate scene changes, and to sacrifice lesser parts — and sometimes the balance of the play — to the star roles. Yet this trend was challenged well before the end of the century by a movement towards presenting the play in simple sets, and using a text that was not only genuine but as complete as possible.

The Romantic movement of the late eighteenth and early nineteenth centuries profoundly influenced attitudes to Shakespeare and consequently Shakesperian production style. The greatest of his early critics, Ben Jonson, [6] Dryden [7] and Doctor Johnson, [8] had deeply admired him, but they had regarded his work as subject to human imperfections, which were legitimate objects of criticism. The new school of Romantic critics, Schlegal [9] in Germany, Coleridge [10] and Hazlitt [11] in England, presented him as almost superhumanly faultless. To them, finding fault with Shakespeare merely exposed the limitations of the critic; or, if they had to admit flaws, they ascribed them to interpolations by inferior authors, or, at worst, to the regrettable influence of Shakespeare's ignorant audience. This attitude influenced the theatre in very varied ways. Reverence for the Bard was an additional motive for returning to his own words, though, as Bernard Shaw [12] pointed out repeatedly near the end of the century, theatrical Bardolatry could go hand in hand with a severely cut text. Some Romantics, like Lamb, [13] thought any performance of Shakespeare inevitably unsatisfactory compared with an imaginative reading. Hazlitt, [14] on the other hand, was the outstanding dramatic critic of his time, and a passionate admirer of Edmund Kean, the greatest of Shakespearian Romantic actors. The chief effect on settings and costumes was the attempt to achieve historical accuracy. One of the marks of Romanticism was its interest in what was historically or geographically remote. In 1813, *Antony and Cleopatra* was produced at Covent Garden with a consistent attempt at historically accurate costumes for both Romans and Egyptians. Eleven years later, Planché achieved even greater accuracy with the medieval costumes he designed for Charles Kemble's production of *King John*. Phelps and Charles Kean continued this trend, and Macready's productions at Covent Garden (1837-1843) combined impressive spectacle with the best acting of the period. As a production style, the historically accurate is still alive. Fortunately, recent examples have usually avoided the ponderousness of their predecessors.

Reaction against overemphasis on spectacle was led in different ways by Frank Benson and William Poel. From 1883 on, Benson's company toured year after year, bringing Shakespeare to many who would otherwise never have seen a good performance of his work, and training many fine actors and actresses who handed on his tradition of verse intelligently spoken before simple and flexible sets. Inspired by the publication in 1888 of the de Witt sketch of the Swan Theatre, Poel founded the Elizabethan Stage Society (1894) whose productions, modelled as closely as possible on Shakespeare's own, have greatly influenced Shakespearian production since. Thus, though the spectacular tradition flourished under Irving at the Lyceum (1878-1899) and then under Tree at the Haymarket and His Majesty's (1878-1912), by the turn of the century, the emphasis was strongly on the primacy of Shakespeare, the whole Shakespeare and nothing but Shakespeare.

This movement reached its pre-war climax in Harley Granville-Barker's famous 1912 season at the Savoy. Actor, dramatist, scholar and producer, Granville Barker is one of the great names in Shakespearian history, not only for the fine examples of his own productions, but for his *Prefaces* to Shakespeare's plays, in which he discussed presentation with the authority of high intelligence allied with wide theatrical experience. Perhaps, like A. C. Bradley, [15] the leading academic Shakespearian of the time, he was inclined to approach the plays too exclusively through the characters, but few actors or producers have turned to him for guidance in vain.

As a producer, perhaps his greatest feat was to take all that was essential from Poel's experiments and make it acceptable in the commercial theatre. Poel painstakingly reconstructed Elizabethan staging: he could not reconstruct an Elizabethan audience. His productions fascinated scholars and students but were too austere to attract the ordinary playgoer. Granville Barker retained all the flexibility of Poel's style but combined it with colourful and attractive sets. He kept the essentials of Shakespearian staging while discarding what was accidental. And this is a principle to which he often recurs in his *Prefaces*.

As we come nearer to our own time, the variety of styles grows faster and faster. The same decade saw Barry Jackson's modern-dress *Hamlet* and Reinhardt's spectacular *A Midsummer Night's Dream*. From 1914 until bomb damage closed it in 1941, the Old Vic was the regular home of Shakespeare at prices that were cheap even for the time. A special tribute is due from all Shakespearians to Robert Atkins, for many years producer at the Vic, at Regent's Park Open Air Theatre, and for two seasons Director at Stratford-upon-Avon. Often handicapped by shortage of funds, he yet trained many fine performers; his productions were always honest and unpretentious. He believed profoundly in the universality of Shakespeare's appeal; and his lifelong devotion was to the Shakespearian word.

Perhaps the most characteristic recent approach is that implied in the title of Professor Jan Kott's brilliant and influential *Shakespeare Our Contemporary*. In sharp contrast to those who saw the plays as pictures of a remote and romantic past, Kott repeatedly emphasizes their relevance to our own condition. What could speak more closely to the twentieth century than the treacheries and cruelties of the History plays? There is no doubt that this approach has given new life not to the Histories alone but to the political element in all the plays. Like many excellent ideas, it can be stressed too exclusively. Some productions have strained too hard to establish contemporary parallels, at the expense of the play as a whole. But the total effect has been enormously revitalizing.

Principles of production

A theatrical production begins with a vision and ends with a performance. The vision may be of a particular moment in the play, a picture of just how it should begin or end, of how some crucial scene should look or sound. It may be suddenly seeing that a particular actor or actress in your company is just right for, say, Malvolio or Juliet. It may arise from a long interest in, or a new exciting encounter with, a play. It may come from either satisfaction or dissatisfaction with a production one has seen. Whatever it is, it must be strong enough to support the producer through all the frustrations and irritations that will inevitably meet him or her between the moment of vision and the first night. To have this strength, it must be based on sympathy with the play, a deep enthusiasm for it, and a realistic appraisal of the resources available: performers, place of performance, audience and finance.

It is important to realize that, important though costumes and settings are, the performers are more important still. The finest costumes and sets imaginable will not save a *Romeo and Juliet* where the lovers are fat and middle-aged or young and good-looking but unable to speak their lines audibly and intelligibly. Neither can one build a satisfactory production around just two or three good performances. This brings up the question of doubling and even trebling the smaller parts. Even major professional companies often do this, but it does involve certain problems. In the nature of things, these smaller parts are normally given to the least experienced or least obviously talented members of the company. One must be careful not to overburden them, remembering that Shakespeare often gave important speeches to minor characters, such as the nameless Gentleman who announces the violent irruption of Laertes into the palace (*Hamlet* IV, 5) or the Clown who brings the asps to Cleopatra (*Antony and Cleopatra*: V, 2). Moreover, doubling and trebling should not obtrude itself on the audience; or the result will be like a demonstration of the Art of Coarse Acting. Finally, one must give enough time for changes of clothes and often of makeup too.

So far I have been assuming a more or less permanent company. If the producer is free to choose more widely, the problems are quite different, but such a producer will probably be experienced enough to know all about them. Casting from a permanent company, amateur or professional, narrows the choice but gives the advantages that arise from the experience of working together in several plays, and, on however modest a level, one is then in a situation similar to Shakespeare's own.

The producer must also carefully consider the place where the play is to be performed. His choice will be limited by availability and cost. In turn, the place will sometimes influence the choice of play. A small acting area makes effective crowd scenes difficult, and so tends to rule out most of the Histories and Roman plays. A big, barn-like hall could accommodate these admirably but might kill the more delicate effects of *Love's Labour's Lost*.

Careful costing is equally essential. Some of the suggestions in Part Two should help to make these as low as possible, but sets and costumes are only some of the expenses involved. All must be estimated carefully and related to reasonable expectations of income.

A producer must consider the composition as well as the size of the audience. Is it likely to be a fair cross-section of an ordinary community, or will it be more specialized, as in the case of a college society? The latter might enjoy the mixture of legalisms, philosophy and bawdry in *Troilus and Cressida*, which might alternately bore and disgust a more staid audience.

The nature of the audience may affect presentation as well as choice. Within living memory, fine actors have presented Hamlet as a gracious and melancholy romantic, as a brilliant and passionate but also morbid and occasionally cruel Renaissance prince, as a somewhat uncouth under-graduate, and as at least assuming grotesque madness. *Henry V* has been produced as a resonant expression of patriotism and as a harsh satire on war and politics. All were impressive: they were not all equally acceptable to every audience. I am not, of course, suggesting for a moment that a producer should distort his own vision simply to please a particular audience. Some of the greatest Shakespearian productions would never have happened if producers had not dared to shock their audiences. It is, however, vital that producer and company should know what they are doing and should consider its probable consequences.

Assuming that all the above questions have been thoroughly discussed and the play chosen, we now come to choose a production style. As I hope to show when examining the ten plays in detail, the play does not automatically determine the style. The deciding factor may be the producer's own response.

Incidentally, for convenience, I have talked and shall continue to talk of a producer, or director.

This in no ways denies the possibility of group production, a method which has created some of the most stimulating Shakespearian productions I have seen — those by the Footsbarn Theatre in Cornwall. If this method is used, unity of approach and the ability to work well together are even more important than usual. Even with a single producer, the whole-hearted support of the company is needed. Just as it is inconceivable that the same producer would be equally happy with both the interpretations of *Henry V* mentioned above, it is inconceivable that the same company should be equally convincing in both of them.

However the production is organized, complete coherence is essential. A successful Shakespearian production is fundamentally an effective way of conveying Shakespeare, or those elements to which a producer and company most vitally respond, to their audience. This emphasis on response may seem too subjective or arrogant, but most of Shakespeare's plays are too rich to have all their meaning expressed in one production; therefore it seems reasonable to concentrate on those elements that appeal most strongly to a particular company, provided that the appeal is genuine and does not lead to distortion. An approach which may convince when it springs from a sincere response to the text may fail totally when it is merely a response to a current trend. One man's insight may be another man's gimmick.

Though choice is wide, it is not unlimited. One may produce *Macbeth* in several types of costume and set, but one must respect the emphasis on darkness. *Twelfth Night* must be produced in such a way that Malvolio's necessary yellow stockings, cross garters and chain of office are not incongruous in the wrong way.

The prime purpose of costume and scenery is to promote that rapport between performer and audience which is the essence of theatrical success. The ultimate question about every costume and every setting is this: does it help the actors to make the audience feel and understand? If the answer is not an unhesitating 'Yes', the producer must think again.

Costume must feel right as well as look right. An actor is not a statue, and a costume, however effective visually, is a hindrance if its wearer cannot comfortably make every move his role demands. Quick changes too must be allowed for; nor should the dressmaker forget the humble but sometimes pressing need for a quick dash to the loo. (I have vivid memories of the difficulties imposed by tights worn with full plate armour in *Richard II* at the Shakespeare Memorial Theatre!) A good costume can strongly reinforce — sometimes help to create — an actor's confidence in himself and his role. Surely everyone who has been connected with a performance that involves special clothes will remember the way morale rose when good costumes were tried on and rehearsed in for the first time. The opposite effect — dismay, even indignation — is fortunately rarer, but when it does occur, it is truly disastrous. This moment of truth is usually too near the first night for radical change, and it is hard indeed to recover from such a blow at such a time.

Good costume can be equally helpful to the audience. Most obviously, it can help them to recognize differences of rank and sometimes differences between groups; between Romans and Egyptians in *Antony and Cleopatra*, for instance. It can visually establish a dramatic clash, as when we first met Hamlet, his solemn black set against the ceremonial magnificence of the Danish court. Paradoxically, it sometimes works by momentarily hindering recognition. In *Twelfth Night*, Viola in her male disguise must dress identically with her twin brother Sebastian, not only because the text says so, but because we should share just enough of the other characters' bewilderment to accept it without losing our own grip on what is really happening. This sort of effect occurs most often in comedy, but in the harshly tragic *Coriolanus* we lose a slight but important shock of recognition if we are sure before he speaks that the muffled figure who enters at the beginning of Act IV, scene 4 is indeed the exiled hero in the city of his enemies.

The essential purpose of sets is the same as that of costume: to bring performance and audience together in responding to Shakespeare. The stage is primarily a place for the performers to act and

for the audience to see and hear them doing so. A beautiful set can be an invaluable asset but one must be careful that it never hinders this primary purpose. Just as the actors must feel at ease in their costumes, so must they feel at ease on their stage. They must be able to carry out all the necessary actions of the play without feeling cramped; and the audience must be able to see them without effort. This means that producer, scenic artist and stage carpenter must make an early and careful on-the-spot inspection of the lines of sight from every part of theatre to every part of the stage, and make sure nothing of importance happens where it cannot be seen comfortably by everyone who is watching.

Enough has been said in the historical chapter about the dangers of over-elaborate sets. Probably most producers today will choose a permanent set, varied perhaps by changes of furniture, hangings and other easily movable decorations. Some may rely largely on a cyclorama. Others may be lucky enough to have a theatre equipped with all the machinery of flies, revolves and stage lifts, reinforced by a full and up-to-date lighting system. These must use their luck with restraint, so that the equipment is always the servant, not the master of their dramatic purpose.

All who read this book doubtless have some special interest in the theatre, and will therefore probably have an extra appreciation of technical points; but, unless we go with the legitimate but limited purpose of studying one of them, they are not our primary concern when we are in the audience. We shall be aware of them. We shall enjoy them, and probably discuss them with those who share our interests; but if they stand out from their proper and subordinate place, we shall know there is something wrong. If we are chiefly aware of the scenery, there is something wrong with scenery. If we are chiefly aware of costumes or the lighting, there is something wrong with them. If, indeed, we are chiefly aware how clever the producer is, there is something wrong with the producer!

PART TWO

Application of principles
to ten selected plays

The following ten plays have been chosen to illustrate the wide range of Shakespeare's work, and also the wide range of possible production styles. The matching of each play with a particular style is consistent with the principles expressed in the previous section, but within that range it has been influenced by a variety of causes.

Before beginning the detailed description of these ten productions, I wish to re-emphasize what I said in the first section: I am *not* asserting that any of the following production styles is the best, still less the only proper, way of presenting the play with which it is matched. I would claim that there is nothing that clashes with the text, and that everything suggested is theatrically practicable — though not necessarily in every situation. I hope that the following sections will help some fellow Shakespearians to continue the long tradition of theatrically realizing the inexhaustible riches of Shakespearian drama.

A late Victorian or Edwardian style

A Midsummer Night's Dream

For a long time, this has been one of Shakespeare's most popular plays. It is very often performed, both by professionals and amateurs; and it is presented in many different ways: simply and elaborately; in many different period styles; indoors and outdoors. It is easy to see why it is so popular. It provides an exceptionally large number and an exceptionally wide variety of good, but not too demanding, acting parts. It combines poetry and romance with several kinds of comedy. There is nothing in it likely to disturb the most sensitive spectator, and Bowdler [1] found little to expurgate from it when in 1818 he published his famous *Family Shakespeare* so much used during the height of Victorian prudery. So, while nobody would class it with Shakespeare's greatest works, it has a wide and enduring appeal, to audiences as well as to performers, though both perhaps often miss its depth.

Like many other Shakespearian plays, the *Dream* suffered a long period of adaptations and then of productions so elaborate that scenery, spectacle and musical effects almost drowned the text. Fortunately, we are now more likely to see at least an attempt to give priority to the author. In one of the penetrating asides that make one wish he had devoted more time to theatrical criticism, G. K. Chesterton commented that the essence of *A Midsummer Night's Dream* was the closeness of the supernatural to the natural, and the ease with which one could meet the other. He added that this was wholly lost if the mortals were as exotically garbed — in magnificent Grecian robes, for example — as the fairies. I would suggest a setting in late nineteenth century England.

Outdoor production This play seems uniquely suited to an outdoor performance. All that is needed is an open space large enough for the actors to act in and for the audience to see them clearly and to hear them comfortably. That is the minimum. An arbour for Titania's bower; some variations of level, and some conveniently placed shrubbery would help greatly, but we could do without them. Audibility is a harder problem, as even a slight breeze can play havoc with sounds. Unless the audience expected is very small indeed, it will be safer to use carefully placed microphones and loudspeakers, despite their tendency to distortion and ill-timed failure. Most gardens that are otherwise suitable will have enough shrubs, trees and flower-beds to hide the equipment. In an outdoor production of the *Dream* furniture is best carried on and off quite openly as required. Fortunately, there is little of it: chairs or a sofa for Theseus and Hippolyta in the first scene and for the performance of 'Pyramus and Thisbe', and in the latter scene, chairs, stools or cushions for the other spectators; a carpenter's bench, some tools and perhaps some rough stools for Quince's workshop — that is really all.

One word of warning before we pass on to the indoor production. Unless the outdoor production is to take place in a remarkably predictable climate, it is essential to provide alternative accommodation under cover. Unless this is available, an outdoor production may well be dismissed as too risky.

Indoor production   If an indoor setting is chosen, there will not be many problems arising from the exact nature of the place. *A Midsummer Night's Dream* is a very adaptable play: it can be performed on an old-fashioned curtained stage, a curtained stage with an apron, an Elizabethan stage, or in the round. For our production, we will choose a curtained stage with an apron. This has certain advantages, but there would be no serious difficulty in adapting it to any of the other stages mentioned. A proscenium arch and curtain fit the nineteenth century, while the addition of the apron has one definite practical advantage: one can set and strike scenery behind the curtain while other scenes are played in front of it.

Settings

If the open-air setting is chosen, there is obviously little to say about scenery: it will be chosen and used; not designed. The pieces of necessary furniture mentioned above must look right and be easily portable: that is all.

Indoors, there is more scope for the designer. The interior of Theseus's palace may be indicated either by a box-set or by hangings. If by hangings, they should be colourful, as the period style limits the colourfulness of the Mortals' costumes, especially for the men. The effect should be a large room in a stately home. The English country-house atmosphere could be simply but clearly conveyed by some occasional tables with silver-mounted family photographs, and perhaps a large fireplace up-centre with logs and a massive set of fire-irons.

If a box-set is preferred, the same effects can be created with more detail. More chairs and sofas, with family portraits of different periods on the walls, including a prominent one of Theseus as a Master of Foxhounds: top-hat, scarlet frock-coat,

white breeches, black riding boots with brown tops; hunting stock, gloves and riding crop. There might be a trophy of arms on the wall as well. These would not only supply atmosphere but build up the picture of Theseus as a man of action as well as authority.

One practical point should be remembered: it must be possible to strike this scene and set Quince's workshop quickly. When Hermia and Lysander are left alone together, thay can easily and naturally move downstage. The curtain can then fall and the scene be changed. There are just over 120 lines for this: enough for a well drilled team but it will need careful planning and a great deal of practice to do it quickly and quietly.

One way of saving time would be to play the workshop scene in front of another curtain, so that the essential changes will be only those that affect the area between this and the front curtain, leaving all upstage to be dealt with at comparative leisure. Only a fairly deep stage would make this device possible. On the other hand, a shallow stage would make an elaborate set for scene 1 uncomfortably crowded anyway, so the problem tends to solve itself.

Except for the curtain, the set for Quince's workshop will be much the same as for an outdoor production, though there could be more tools, and pieces of timber, worked and unworked. The curtain itself could depict a wall and window, and possibly shelves with more tools and timber.

Act II, scene 1 can be played on the apron while the main forest scene is being set behind it. Once set, this can remain until near the end of IV. 1. When the court party leave, the curtain could come down, leaving Bottom to wake up and deliver his soliloquy on the apron stage. While he is doing this, Quince's workshop can be set in front of its own curtain, and much of the court interior behind that. It may be objected that Bottom went to sleep in Titania's bower, which can hardly, in this style of production, be left on stage during the last two scenes. Fortunately, like Bottom himself earlier in the play, we 'have a device to make all well'. During the business of removing the ass's head, it will be quite easy to move Bottom to a convenient situation downstage. Another solution is a dim-out — nearly always

The four lovers

preferable to a black-out in Shakespeare — during which the bower can be struck.

Obviously it is impossible to complete setting the court interior during the short second scene of Act IV, but the nature of the next scene — amateur theatricals in the palace — permits, almost demands, a preliminary rearrangement of furniture. The final part of this can be carried out quite openly by court servants. The vital points are that 'Pyramus and Thisbe' must have the apron, so as to give the audience full benefit of all the nuances as well as the broader effects; and that the stage spectators should be near enough for their comments to be heard by the audience as well as by the Mechanicals. This set remains to the end, though with different lighting for the fairies' ceremonial blessing after the Mortals have gone to bed.

The main forest scene, though the longest in the play, and the one most deeply involved with its dreamlike quality, is fundamentally simple. All we need is the impression of trees stretching far beyond the audience's range of vision; of the hawthorn brake for the Mechanicals' tiring-house, and of Titania's bower or bank. A good backcloth, helped by imaginative lighting, can give us the forest. The hawthorn brake has often, and successfully, been indicated off-stage. Titania's bower is more demanding, as Oberon describes it in considerable detail:

> I know a bank where the wild thyme blows,
> Where oxlips and the nodding violet grows,
> Quite over-canopied with luscious woodbine,
> With sweet musk-roses and with eglantine;
> There sleeps Titania sometime of the night.

One may accept his poetic description as calling a picture to our imaginations that no scenic display could live up to. In some production styles, this is what we would do; but here we are using a somewhat more visual approach. We need not worry about the minute botanical accuracy of the décor, but we must avoid any clashes that would arouse critical disbelief in the spectator. A profusion of the appropriate flowers, walling and partly roofing the bower, will serve us well. The bank will simply be stage grass draped over a base that is firm enough to keep its shape during the action, and

yet soft enough for the performers who have to use it. Titania and Bottom are on it for quite a long time.

The need to separate different parts of the forest and the people temporarily in them, can be met either by placing artificial shrubs or by concentrating light in the appropriate areas.

Costume

Theseus's exclamation at the beginning of Act I. 1. — 'but O, methinks, how slow This old moon wanes' — suggests that this is an evening scene. All the characters, therefore, should be in the evening dress of the period. This differed in many respects from that of today. The difference are most obvious for the ladies, but the men's clothes must be accurate too. Men of this rank would be wearing tail-coats, and the tails should be wider than those of today. The waistcoat is black instead of white. The collar is starched and high, either with ends overlapping and going straight up under the chin, or with points turned out in the butterfly style. The second style could be used by the younger men, though contemporary pictures do not show a clear correlation between age and collar-style. In any case, the collar shows the whole of the white tie, which was less butterfly-shaped than ours, and must at least *look* as though it has been tied by hand. The shirt, of which a great deal shows, is starched. The excellence of his starching was one of the chief prides of the dandy, so both Lysander and Demetrius must have shirt, collar and cuffs that are stiff and gleaming. The others' must be in good condition, especially Theseus's but can be less obtrusive. It would be in order, though not necessary, to mark his rank by the collar or sash of an Order of Knighthood, real or fictitious. The collar would consist of a coloured ribbon round his neck, with a gold and jewelled medallion hanging on his chest. The sash would be much broader and would cross from one shoulder to a tassel by the opposite hip. All the gentlemen's costumes are fundamentally similar, so minor differences would be significant. Philostrate, who should be conceived as a confidential secretary, should be more subdued; Egeus slightly shabby in a casually aristocratic way, perhaps showing signs of haste in his dress.

Hippolyta and Theseus

The Mechanicals; Starveling, Flute, Snout and Snug

Bottom and Quince

The ladies too would have a common basic pattern, but with more variety in detail and in colour. A fairly close-fitting bodice over an ankle-length skirt cut tight in front and loose behind was the common ground. The sleeves could be long or short, close-fitting or puffed at the shoulders, and there was a wide range of permissible degrees of décolleté, generally more being allowed for a married or mature woman than for a young one. Hippolyta, therefore, would wear a noticeably lower-cut bodice than Hermia. White or cream and gold seem a suitably striking and regal colour combination for her; a white or cream background with lavish gold trimmings, plus such jewellery as the designer fancies and the director approves. Whether she should wear long or short sleeves may depend on whether her arms would indicate Amazonian prowess.

Pale green and white would suggest Hermia's fresh youth: a green bodice with green skirt showing a white centre panel would be a suitable way of combining the colours. Her bodice might modestly come right up to a lace-trimmed collar. Dove greys and violet would suggest Helena's less incisive character. Both must wear jewellery less striking than Hippolyta's.

In the forest scenes, Lysander and Demetrius should wear Norfolk suits; rather long jackets, knickerbockers, knitted woollen stockings and heavy brogues. They would still wear ties and stiff collars. Their headgear should be shaped like a cricket cap, but, like their suits, of checked tweed. These two young men are not very sharply distinguished so actors will need all the help clothes can give to establish their characters. Lysander seems definitely the more dashing, and a bolder check with brighter colours will underline this, though one must be careful not to suggest vulgarity. Demetrius's less flamboyant nature can be suggested by smaller checks and a quieter pattern.

Hermia and Helena will change their silk evening gowns for tweed skirts and blouses. A red cloak would bring out Hermia's fiery nature, while Helena could wear dove-grey. Both could wear velvet 'Robin Hood' hats with feathers matching their cloaks.

The Athenian Mechanicals must wear the sort of clothes proper to skilled artisans of the time: jackets and trousers of fustian or corduroy, flannel shirts and white-spotted bandana neckerchiefs, and high-crowned bowler hats. In his own workshop, Quince could wear an apron instead of his coat.

Again, differences in character can be helped by dress. Bottom's bowler could have a curlier brim and he could wear a colourful waistcoat. Quince is clearly the intellectual of the group, and he could show this by wearing a dark tie instead of a bandana. Flute could suggest a hesitant foppishness with a soft, even floppy hat instead of a bowler. Starveling might wear a rusty frockcoat over a shabby suit. Snout, as the player cast for Wall, must be a fairly big man, and a loud checked waistcoat with a heavy brass watchchain could suggest this. Snug's self-effacing nature calls for neat, quiet clothes, perhaps with a faintly clerical air — a white neckerchief instead of a bandana.

The text clearly indicates what Wall, the Lion and the Man in the Moon are to wear for 'Pyramus and Thisbe'. Pyramus should have a plumed helmet, breastplate, cloak, sword and shield, and leggings worn under a skirt. Thisbe should wear a long, shapeless dress and a white cloak. As the Prologue, Quince would wear his best suit of Sunday black. As prompter, he would have his script, and perhaps a pot of red paint and a brush to daub 'gore' on Thisbe's cloak. All the play costumes should have an obviously home-made appearance.

For the hunting scene (IV. 1), Theseus must be dressed as an MFH, as for his portrait (see page 27). Hippolyta would wear the black hunting habit of the period: long-skirted, with top-hat and veil, which she can draw back for the scene. Alternatively, and perhaps better for the Queen of the Amazons, she too could wear the scarlet coat of an MFH. One production of the *Dream* I saw had a most effective device whereby both Theseus and Hippolyta had a sort of rocking-horse tied to their waists, so that the upper halves of their own bodies came up through the middle. These artificial horses were so constructed — presumably on stiff wire frames — that every move of the 'riders' made them bounce gently in a most entertaining manner. This is certainly a possibility to consider.

When we come to the fairies, we have to make

Titania, Oberon, Puck and the Fairies

a sharp contrast between them and the Mortals, and to make significant distinctions within the fairy group itself. Oberon and Titania are rulers of a fairy empire that stretches from India to England, so their appearance demands an exotic elegance. Smallness and daintiness are essential for Titania's attendants. Puck, that 'lob of spirits', needs a costume that expresses his earthier, more rustic nature.

Dark green tights, ballet-type shoes, a tight-fitting gold shirt, either closed to the throat and ending in a high collar, or open to the waist with a turned-back and stiffened collar would be a good basis for Oberon's costume, conveying both elegance and the slightly sinister quality he shows in his treatment of Titania. He could also wear a spiky gold crown, and a dark green cloak with a gold lining. The lining could be displayed most of the time, but he could sweep the cloak round him so as to merge with the forest background when he says, 'I am invisible.' (II. 1. 186).

Titania should have the same pattern of crown, lighter green tights, and a low, tight top, with jewelled and stiffened collar turned back from the top. Her cloak could be lined with silver. Tights instead of a skirt would point the contrast between her and the Mortal females.

Shakespeare has given us clear hints about the four named fairies. Peaseblossom and Mustardseed should have leaf-green as the basic colour of their bodytights, but Peaseblossom's should be plain, while Mustardseed's should have the veined pattern of the mustard plant's leaf. These two green backgrounds can be colourfully decorated with the appropriate flowers or flower colours: yellow for Mustardseed; yellow, light purple and pink for Peaseblossom. There is some botanical confusion of peas here, but this is allowable in a fairy.

Puck's costume should combine the rusticity of Robin Goodfellow with a reminder that he is also the King's confidential servant. For this, I have taken ideas from what we know of two famous clowns just before Shakespeare's time: Will Sommers, jester to King Henry VIII, and Dick Tarlton, at whose death in 1588, Spenser wrote

> With whom all joy and joly meriment
> Is also deaded, and in dolour drent.

Court accounts tell us Sommers's usual livery was a 'coate of grene cloth', plain or guarded with velvet. It seems to have been Tarlton who created the special association between a stage comic and the word 'clown', whose primary meaning was simply 'countryman'. Combining Sommers's green with Tarlton's [3] jerkin and breeches, we have a satisfactory costume for Puck. He may be bareheaded or wear a buttoned cap, like Tarlton's. He may wear boots or go barefoot.

Lighting

Most of the lighting of *A Midsummer Night's Dream* is easy to visualize but the execution needs care, especially in deciding where light is to be concentrated and the precise speed at which lights should be raised and lowered. Very slight differences in focus and tempo can produce very big differences in effect. The principle is to avoid anything harsh or sudden.

Spots are even more important in the forest night, where they have to create the feeling of night without ever hiding the action from the audience. Fade-ins and dim-outs are invaluable devices.

In the last scene lighting must

> Through the house give glimmering light.

At its fullest during most of the scene, it will dim to a glow as the Mortals leave the stage. A single spot can light Puck for his first speech. The producer can choose between several effects for the speeches of Oberon and the fairy song and dance. Much will depend on how elaborate the latter are to be. They may be a major feature of the finale or there may be no song, and a procession instead of a dance — a good procession with the fairies carrying torches as they weave a pattern on the dimly lit stage is far better than an over-ambitious dance that does not quite succeed. This is one of the rare cases where the audience does not need to see in detail all that is going on. They can be deeply satisfied by the sense of movement, swirling or stately, only half-seen in the glimmering light as the fairies bless the house and Puck speaks the epilogue.

A neo-classical style

The Comedy of Errors

The Comedy of Errors, Shakespeare's most interesting essay in farce, is based on a famous Latin example of the genre, the *Menaechmi* of Plautus. Yet, though Shakespeare added to the improbabilities of Plautus's story by having two pairs of identical twins instead of one, and by exploiting the possibilities of this situation to the full, he produced something more than a mere farce. There is genuine feeling in the story of Aegeon and his quest, which foreshadows similar quests and reunions in Shakespeare's last plays. The bewilderment produced by mistaken identity is farcically entertaining to the audience, but the characters involved feel genuine fear and confusion about their identity.

Casting presents problems: however much costume and lighting help, one must have two pairs of similar-looking actors for the audience to accept the repeated confusions of identity. If these problems can be solved, a production of *The Comedy of Errors* should be enjoyed by all concerned, and lead to a better appreciation of a play that has often been underrated. At worst, it has been dismissed as trivial prentice work; at best, it has seemed a jolly romp, where every licence with the text is permissible. Some productions of this sort have been enjoyable and commercially successful, and it would be harshly pedantic to object too strongly. Nevertheless, the play deserves more respect.

Setting

One important reason for including *The Comedy of Errors* is its striking suitability for a distinctive production style, which we may call the neo-classical. This is based on the illustrations to fifteenth and sixteenth century editions of Plautus and Terence; illustrations which the artists seem to have believed reproduced the customs of the Roman theatre. The basic equipment was an arcade set at the back of the stage. In this were as many doors or curtains and, if necessary, windows, as the action required. Most of the action took place on the main stage — which represented a street or market place — or at the doors, which represented entrances to houses. In *The Comedy of Errors*, three doors and some windows are needed: one for the house of Antipholus of Ephesus; one for the Courtezan's; the third for the Priory. Antipholus's house is called the Phoenix, which indicates an appropriate sign, clearly visible. Because of its major importance it should be in the centre. This will also help the staging of Act III, scene 1, which would be easier still if this house had a projecting bay. In addition to its practical value, it is warranted by a fifteenth century illustration to Terence.

There must be a marked contrast between the Priory and the Courtezan's house. Line 116 in III. 1 names her house the Porpentine (the form of

33

porcupine that Shakespeare always used). This gives it a sign, which could be rather gaudy, and the meretricious effect could be heightened by a bright door and showy window curtains. Any easily recognizable religious symbol could indicate the Priory. I should favour a statue of Madonna and Child, as the image of the traditionally perfect woman would underline the contrast with the traditionally sinful woman on the other side. It would also harmonize with the reunion of mother and child which takes place right in front of the Priory.

The only remaining question about the set is whether there should be a practical upper storey and window for Act III, scene 1. At the beginning of this scene, Antipholus of Ephesus arrives at his house with his guests, and his servant, Dromio of Ephesus. The audience knows that his long lost identical twin is already in the house dining with its mistress, Adriana, who has mistaken him for her husband. The parallel servant twin, Dromio of Syracuse, is also in the house, acting as porter, with strict instructions to 'let none enter'. There follows a scene of cross-purposes, insults and threats, which ends with Antipholus of Ephesus taking his guests off to dine at the Porpentine. During the exchanges, those outside the Phoenix

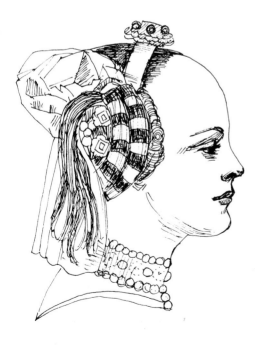

are obviously on the main stage, at the door, and cleary visible. But what about those inside? Are they visible too or do we just hear their voices? If they are visible, for how long? And where are they? Does the audience see them through an open window or half-door on the ground floor, or at an upper window?

Voices alone tend to be unsatisfactory and confusing for more than a very short scene, so the producer will probably want to show the characters in the house for most of the battle of words. One solution is to have the door of the Phoenix on one side of the bay, so that the centre and the other side can, for this scene anyway, be clearly seen. If the interior floor is raised and a half-door is used, the spectators on the door side of the auditorium should be able to see. Admittedly, this is not convincing in naturalistic terms. Why does nobody look in or out and notice at least one of the identical twins? Fortunately, both the play itself and the production style are non-realistic, so this need not worry us.

Nevertheless, some might feel happier to use a window set above the bay. If this is level with the back wall of the arcade, the projection of the bay

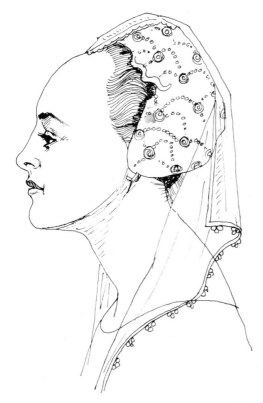

wrist-length undersleeves. Collars were varied: wide, narrow, tight, open, round, square. Other men wore tunic and hose with an open cloak, long or short. Theatrically and, so far as we can see, historically, the long robe seems better suited to the older and more stolid citizens; the open cloak with tunic and hose to the younger and more fashionable. Contemporary pictures show a wide variety of hats too: skull caps, square caps with ear-pieces, wide brimmed hats with crowns or trimmed with fur. Servants wore thigh or knee length tunics, and hose. Boots normally indicated a traveller: a useful convention to the producer.

Women wore long, loose-skirted dresses, often showing a tighter skirt underneath. Tops might be either square or V-shaped. These dresses were sometimes laced at the back of the neck to show a contrasting undergarment. Ladies of high rank often wore richly brocaded dresses sometimes in spectacularly contrasting colours. Women of lower rank wore fairly loose dresses of plain material, with a cord under the breasts and sometimes also just above the hips, presumably to raise them to

can suggest that it hides those on ground level from those above.

For the rest, a plain open stage will suffice, with an entrance at each side. The First Folio has an interesting stage direction at IV. 1. 85: 'Enter Dromio Sira (Syracusan) from the Bay.' Though we cannot be sure that Shakespeare consistently associated one side of his stage with the bay and the other with the town, as Peter Alexander suggests, [1] it is a helpful hint to a producer. Spectators may not always be conscious of such associations but they can have a useful dramatic effect for all that.

Costume

Fortunately, the late fifteenth century editions of Plautus and Terence that suggested the scenery for this production also show a number of suitable costumes, though any paintings or drawings of the period may supply valuable information and ideas. Some men wore ankle-length robes, belted and often with short wide sleeves showing tight,

The twins Dromios and Antipholuses

Adriana Luciana and the Abbess

about half-calf length for ease of movement when working. Italian paintings of the courtesans of the period show them wearing dresses similar in general to those of rich ladies but noticeably lower cut. One portrait of a courtesan shows her in a plain but diaphanous top reaching diagonally from her right shoulder so as to expose her left breast. Both headgear and footwear are noteworthy. One courtesan wears a turban over a close-fitting jewelled cap, the turban being bound with a wreath of flowers. Others wear a kind of skull cap perched on top of the head. All, incidentally, wear a false front of yellow hair, stiffened with gum and dyed bright yellow. The effect is of metal ringlets. Shoes were often wedge-type, and very high.

When we turn from the fifteenth century in general to the particular needs of our play, the first consideration is that the two Antipholuses must be dressed exactly alike, as must their servants. Aegeon's account of his history in Act I establishes that all four were the same age, twenty-three. It is equally clear that both his sons should be dressed as fashionable young gentlemen. A suitable basic pattern would be a tunic, shoulder cloak and elegantly tight-fitting hose. The upper garments could be in contrasting colours, plain or ornamented, while borders and linings give further opportunities for decoration. In choosing from the wide variety of historically suitable hats, one must be careful to avoid anything that will hide the actor's face or make him ridiculous to a modern audience. Though the Antipholuses are placed in absurd positions, they are not absurd in themselves. In the long run, it is actually funnier, as well as more deeply interesting, to see quite serious characters taking themselves seriously, while caught in a tangle of misunderstandings.

The two Dromios can wear the typical servant's short tunic and hose. Though their clothes must be inferior to their masters', they should be of reasonably good material and cut: their appearance should reflect credit on their masters.

Solinus, the Duke of Ephesus, appears only in his official capacity. A long robe of some rich but sombre colour, deeply trimmed with fur, and gathered with a broad sash would suit him well. A cap of maintenance and a staff or wand of office

would complete his costume. Alternatively, the suggestion of an Italian setting, added to recurrent references to the sea and sea traffic might justify an approximation to the costume of a Doge of Venice. This would include a cloak with elaborate floral decorations, high and tight to the throat, with a floral design on gold. A special feature is the characteristically shaped cap with its horn-like protuberance at the back.

Aegeon's character and situation call for a distinctively sober garb. The long robe gathered at the waist, perhaps with wide sleeves revealing tight undersleeves, all in sombre colours, would be appropriate. A square cap with earflaps would go well with this. As a traveller, he would presumably wear boots, though these would be barely visible under his long robe.

There are three merchants in the play, in addition to Aegeon. Their dress should help the audience to distinguish them, yet there should also be a generic likeness. The two anonymous merchants (appearing in I. 2 and IV. 1) should both have robes similar to Aegeon's, but brighter. Balthasar, as a friend or at least a social acquaintance of Antipholus of Ephesus, should probably be younger and more fashionably dressed. Tunic, hose and shoulder cloak could give this impression, and a similar costume, with variations of colour and ornament, would suit Angelo the goldsmith. He might advertise his wares by an ostentatious display of gold jewellery.

Doctor Pinch, the schoolmaster acting as exorcist, could wear a black cassock under a cloak like the present Oxford or Cambridge MA gown. He should wear white clerical bands and, in view of the still close conection between the clerical and scholastic professions, his headgear should at least suggest a biretta.

Of the women, Emilia the Abbess presents no problems. Any nun-like dress will serve. There is no need to keep strictly to the habit of a particular order. Adriana and her sister, Luciana, should be similarly dressed on the lines suggested above. Adriana's might be a little richer and yet more sober to stress her status as a married woman. Incidentally, both might adopt the historically appropriate hair-style, which aimed at heightening the forehead by dragging the hair tightly back; sometimes indeed even plucking it.

While we need not take literally Dromio of Syracuse's description of the servant, sometimes named Luce and sometimes Nell, she should clearly be short and fat. Her loose fitting dress must make the most of this.

Props

For this style of production, furniture is non-existent. One hand-prop, however, is vital: the chain or carcanet which causes so much confusion and quarrelling. It should be large enough for every member of the audience not only to see it, but to register its importance.

Lighting

Clear, bright light is needed throughout, with slight dimming in the last act, to indicate the approach of evening, and to give a mellowness to the reunion and reconciliation that end the play.

A production in the round with Elizabethan costumes

Twelfth Night

As we began by emphasizing the variety of styles in which Shakespeare may be staged, we certainly need one example of production in the round, and *Twelfth Night* seems a very suitable play to choose. Dr Hotson has argued strongly in 'The First Night of *Twelfth Night*' that this was the original style. Whether he was correct is a matter of learned controversy: we are concerned here with the practical question of performance. From this aspect, our chosen style is cheap and flexible, and gives close contact with the audience, a particular advantage in this play, with its combination of delicate poetry and intricate word-play. The avoidance of scenic naturalism parallels the play's avoidance of dramatic naturalism.

There have long been differing opinions about the essential qualities of *Twelfth Night*. The prevailing view has seen it as the apogee of Shakespeare's romantic comedy; a masterly blend of poetry, love and several kinds of comedy, where obstacles exist only to be overcome, threats are not to be taken seriously, and even false imprisonment and broken heads are painless jokes. There has long been opposition to this. Its earliest form was to take the gulling of Malvolio as a painful humiliation inflicted on a good man for doing his duty. More recently, Auden felt Shakespeare was in no mood for comedy when he wrote *Twelfth Night*. [1] and Kott found it bitter despite its apparent gaiety. [2] Both views seem to omit some-

thing, but the former, despite the danger of sentimental superficiality, seems nearer the truth.

Certainly *Twelfth Night* does pose problems of interpretation. One confronts us at the very beginning. How are we to see Orsino? Many regard him as a slightly absurd dreamer, playing the part of the forlorn lover rather than genuinely in love with Olivia. While there is an important element of romantic make-believe in Orsino, it should not be exaggerated. Certainly what is comic in him must not destroy his dignity and so make him an unworthy match for Viola. His love for Olivia was rather unreal, but it was not entirely empty. His wooing of her by embassy was normal for a sixteenth century ruler, and does not necessarily imply half-heartedness. The change of his affections from Olivia to Viola is far less sudden than Romeo's from Rosaline to Juliet. His attraction to Cesario-Viola is marked from the beginning of Act I, scene 4. From then on, the audience, who are in the secret of Cesario's true identity and sex, can see that it is only her 'masculine, usurp'd attire' that blinds Orsino to the real nature of his feelings for her. As soon as she is revealed as a woman, he recognizes his love for her.

Olivia presents similar problems of balance. Like Orsino, she progresses from illusion to knowledge — a perennial theme of comedy, and one prominent in *Twelfth Night* — but she too must preserve dignity and charm. She is often played

41

noticeably older than Viola. This may be unavoidable, but it does unbalance the play, especially when she woos Cesario and contracts herself to Sebastian.

Malvolio has long been a bone of contention. Is he a loyal and conscientious servant, whose very virtues provoke his ribald inferiors, and whose serious-mindedness betrays him to their cruel mockery? Or is he a pompous kill-joy, whose misuse of authority deserves all the humiliations to which his inflated ambition exposes him? Surely both are partially, but only partially, true. He is conscientious. It is his duty as Steward to keep order in Olivia's household, and to suppress the untimely rowdiness of Sir Toby and his crew. Olivia regards him highly, but she also warns him early (I.5. 85-90) against self-love, touchiness and lack of humour, the precise faults that bring all his troubles. His rebukes may be deserved but he relishes them too much. His contempt for the Fool appears gratuitous, and is so tactlessly worded that it reflects on Olivia herself, stinging her to sharp retort. Even before he reads the forged letter, he is dreaming of marrying Olivia and lording it over the rest of the household. At the end, though gulled, he is unbroken in spirit, though also, it seems, in vanity and anger. In the circumstances, Orsino's 'Pursue him and entreat him to a peace;' is as near reconciliation as one can hope for. If Shakespeare had wished us to sympathize deeply with Malvolio at the end, it is surprising that he should reveal that the Sea Captain who had befriended Viola was 'now in durance at Malvolio's suit' immediately before we hear Malvolio's own protests. Why should Shakespeare have gone out of his way to present such a pleasant character as Malvolio's victim unless he wanted to qualify our sympathy with Malvolio's own sufferings?

Feste is another problem. He is often regarded as a very melancholy jester indeed, beginning in Olivia's bad books and ending solitary and out of a job. The vein of melancholy is there, but this picture is far too gloomy. He quickly talks himself back into Olivia's favour. He is in demand at the Duke's palace. In fact, everybody likes him, except Malvolio. And there is not a scrap of evidence that he is dismissed at the end.

One has seen such odd portrayals of Olivia's household that a few comments may be helpful, especially for a production in Elizabethan dress, which calls for some observance of Elizabethan conventions. Sir Toby is not a very reputable character but he is Olivia's kinsman, though the precise relationship is arguable; so he must not be too much a buffoon. To a lesser degree, this also applies to Sir Andrew. His surname of Aguecheek is usually taken to imply thinness, and he and Sir Toby are often portrayed as belonging to the old tradition of pairing a thin comic with a fat one. The text gives no clear evidence that Sir Toby is fat, but fatness is certainly in keeping with his way of life. Maria, as the waiting-gentlewoman to a lady of Olivia's rank, would have a high enough social status herself to be an acceptable match for Sir Toby. Fabian's status is doubtful, so he can be played either as a gentleman of the household or as a servant of distinctly lower rank. The references that favour the high rank are more numerous but not decisive.

The remaining characters pose no problems of interpretation, which is far from saying they are easy to act well. Viola's difficulties, for example, are of execution rather than conception. The combination of deep feeling with resourcefulness and wit is easy to imagine but hard to project satisfactorily. It is, of course, important not to play for cheap laughs about her sex, especially in the scenes with Olivia. As usual with Shakespeare, careful study of the words and faithfulness to them is the best way to success.

Setting

For this production, we envisage an acting area at floor level, completely surrounded by seating for the spectators. Seating in tiers is best for giving a clear view to a large audience. Smaller audiences have been satisfactorily accommodated in school halls which have a central well with a higher level on all four sides. Here, the well has accommodated one or two rows of spectators as well as the performers, while the rest of the audience sat on the forward parts of the upper level. If raised seating is impracticable, the acting area must be raised to be clearly visible to spectators at floor level.

The main scenery consists of two mansions,

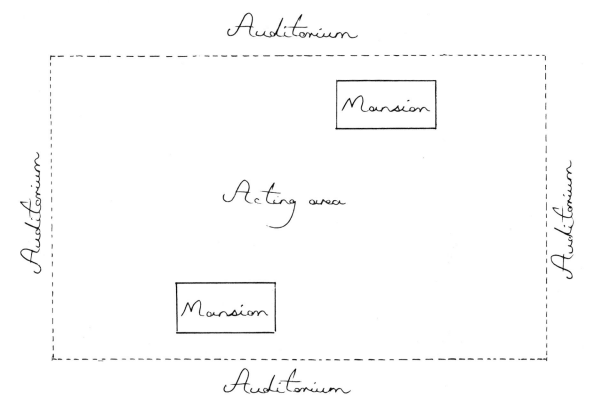

Auditorium

Mansion

Acting area

Mansion

Auditorium

Auditorium

Auditorium

one representing Orsino's palace, the other, Olivia's. These would consist of light metal frames hung with curtains or walled with painted canvas on all four sides. The roofs could be domed or pyramid-shaped. Both they and the walls or curtains could be richly coloured or comparatively plain. The advantage of curtains is that they can be completely drawn to show the interior of the mansions. Canvas walls lack this advantage but admit of more elaborate pictorial effects. If these walls were immovable, except for the necessary two doors in each mansion, some clearly interior scenes would have to be played immediately outside the mansions. This would hardly matter in our non-representational style. One could make the best of both worlds by having the canvas walls hooked to the frames so that they can be quickly removed and replaced as required, either by suitable members of the cast or by stage staff appropriately dressed.

What about interior scenes where a fairly large number are on at the same time? Won't the mansions be either unwieldily large or uncomfortably crowded? This problem is easily solved by our flexible and non-representational style. Take the opening scene, in the Duke's palace. We begin with Orsino himself, Curio and other lords, with musicians attending. Half-way through, Valentine enters. Only three speaking parts, but the lords and musicians could easily swell the total to nine or more. If Orsino sits on a large ornamental chair in the mansion, with the curtains drawn back, the mansion will be transformed into a canopied state. Curio and the other lords can sit on cushions or stand around him, still within the mansion, while the musicians stand or sit on the ground just outside, or perhaps offstage. A similar device may be used in Act I, scene 5, where Olivia's house has to accommodate a large number. Her mansion, fully open, could hold the speaking characters in the early part of the scene, while her mute attendants stand at the back or outside. When she receives 'Orsino's embassy', her chair, in turn, would become a canopied state. We can treat most of the

Orsino Cesario/Viola and attendant

other interiors in the same way. One obvious exception is Act IV, scene 2, where Malvolio is imprisoned in a dark room. Here, Olivia's mansion must be completely closed, so that we can only hear Malvolio's voice from 'within'. That is, the mansion now represents one room in the house, while the space immediately outside is another room or a passage.

Except when open to show an interior, both mansions will be shut. Orsino's palace should be curtained or walled in gold, with his punning cognizance of a bear ('Orsino' means 'bear') in white on black. Olivia's could be silver and black.

Props

Furniture and other stage dressing are important but simple. Both Orsino and Olivia need a large chair with arms and a high back, carved and perhaps gilded. Each would have a velvet cushion; red with a gold fringe for him, green with a silver fringe for her. Stools and a table set with drinking vessels would serve Sir Toby and Sir Andrew in Act 1, scene 3 and Act II, scene 3; the stools and table could appear in Act III, scene 2. They could be set in Olivia's mansion. If this is too cramped, they could be set partly inside and partly out, thus using the flexibility of the style.

Olivia's garden can be indicated by a deliberately artificial looking box tree or hedge, set and struck as required. Alternatively, each of the onlookers in the letter scene can carry his own miniature tree; a method which worked very well in an interesting recent production at the Northcott Theatre in Exeter. For the rest, Shakespeare's words and the audience's imagination can paint the scene.

When the performers are off, they may either sit round the edge of the acting area or exit out of the auditorium.

Costume

We chose Elizabethan costume because it fits both action and atmosphere so well, but our basic setting, altered in detail and decoration, could serve a performance quite differently dressed. Many producers have seen Shakespeare's Illyria as a never-never land, and have accordingly dressed it to avoid suggesting any particular place or time. Some fine imaginative effects may be gained this way, especially if due attention is paid to colour symbolism.

Orsino, young, princely, with a hint of bear-like ferocity to give strength to his elegance and charm, needs red and gold as his dominant colours. He should wear a gold doublet, jewelled with rubies, with red picadils, over similarly decorated trunk hose, slashed to display contrasting red. Below these, plain white hose would display his legs to the best advantage. (If the actor's legs are not very shapely, the historically accurate division into canions and netherstocks would help to disguise this unfortunate fact.) His gold shoes would be slashed and jewelled. A large medallion would hang on his chest, suspended from a chain of gold and rubies. His cloak would be red, gold-lined. His hat red with a jewelled band and an ostrich plume.

Sebastian must wear exactly the same as Viola in her Cesario disguise. I suggest that the dominant colours should be green and violet; green for youth, hope and love; violet for her name and as symbolizing the sadness that hangs over her until the end. So for both, the doublet could be of green with violet decoration and violet sleeves. The trunk hose could have green panes showing violet underneath; their hose, white canions with green netherstocks, over green shoes. Their cloaks should be violet, green-lined, and their hats of matching violet. Pearls should be their jewels, as precious beings snatched from the sea.

Olivia's clothes should combine the early emphasized mourning for her brother with Orsino's ecstatic recognition that 'now heaven walks on earth'. A black, hooded, silver-lined cloak, worn over a dress of azure blue would satisfy these requirements. The azure dress would be worn over a Spanish farthingale with diamond and silver clasps. Wide, open sleeves, lined with green silk, would show silver undersleeves.

Except for Act I, scene 2, Viola will wear the clothes described for Sebastian. On her first appearance, she can wear a green sea-cloak over a plain violet travelling dress.

Sir Toby's basic colours should be crimson and brown. Brown suggests earthiness; crimson

Sir Toby, Sir Andrew and Feste

Maria, Olivia and Malvolio

both a drinker's complexion and a crude virility. Doublet, trunk hose, canions and netherstocks, and a short cloak could display these colours. His 'these clothes are good enough to drink in; and so be these boots too:' (I. 3. 9-11) gives useful information.

Sir Andrew seems a much less likely Taurus than Sir Toby (See I. 3. 128-130) but one can picture him in such Taurean colours as pink and blue. These, skilfully used, could enhance the thinness his name implies and the straight, flax-like hair on which Sir Toby comments in Act I, scene 3, line 96. Given Sir Toby's regular deception of his friend, his compliment to 'the excellent constitution of the leg' is almost certainly satirical. Plain pink tights, worn under short trunk hose, would emphasize their thinness. A blue and pink doublet, under a pink-lined blue cloak, would show him off well.

Feste's 'I did impeticos thy gratillity' (ie I put your tip in my petticoat) indicates he wears the fool's motley coat of grey-green associated with Robert Armin, who probably played Feste in the earliest performances.

Until his gulling, Malvolio is most suitably dressed in black: cloak, doublet, trunk hose, stockings and shoes. The only touches of colour could be a white plume on his high black hat and the silver of his Steward's chain of office. After he has read the forged letter, he must wear yellow stockings and cross-garters. (The cross-garters are often misunderstood. In the sixteenth century, they did not reach all the way down the legs, but simply went round the leg below the knee, crossed behind, and were tied in front, above the knee.)

These are the only changes clear from the text, but Malvolio might try to brighten his whole appearance with jewellery, black and yellow doublet and trunk hose, matching gloves and a yellow-plumed hat. It is a question of what the producer considers at once the funnier and the more in keeping: cross garters and yellow stockings contrasting with the accustomed sombreness of his usual garments, or a total transformation into Malvolio's idea of a dashing lover.

Orsino's courtiers would dress as fashionable young men, fit attendants to a prince who was also a romantic young lover. The Duke's prophecy that Cesario will prove a more successful ambassador of love than a messenger 'of more grave aspect' (I. 4. 25-27) could imply that Valentine, the previous and unsuccessful ambassador, was noticeably older, but it is uncertain. Any servants of lower rank could wear a livery of red and gold stripes with the bear badge, white on black, on the breast.

Similarly, Olivia's unnamed attendants could wear a livery of black and silver stripes. This leaves Maria. She must be dressed as a lady. Taking a hint from Sir Toby's reference to her as 'the youngest wren of nine', (III. 2. 62) her prevailing colour could be a warm brown, perhaps open in front to show a cream undergown.

Lighting

This can be very straightforward. Spots and floods can be at floor level, on stands, or hung from the ceiling. Clear, warm light is the main essential for the outdoor scenes. For the night scenes, light should be concentrated on the areas where the action is occurring.

All changes should take place openly. If the producer wants to mask them, dim-outs will serve his turn. Sudden blackouts are much too harsh.

Music

Twelfth Night makes very special demands for variety and excellence of music. Even more than most of Shakespeare's plays, it reminds us that Elizabethan England was famous for its music throughout Europe. It begins with an invocation to the power of music and ends with Feste's song. In between, vocal and instrumental music are seldom absent long. Some of this may be off-stage or mimed, but Feste must be able to sing his own songs. As we are using Elizabethan dress, Elizabethan music would be most fitting. There is very helpful detailed information, with music, in the New Arden edition of *Twelfth Night*.

A picture stage with Elizabethan costume

Love's Labour's Lost

This early comedy combines a romantic plot with brilliant word-play and topical satire on the intellectual coteries of Shakespeare's early manhood. Several critics believe that Shakespeare was trying to support his patron, the Earl of Southampton, and the Earl's patron, the Earl of Essex, against the latter's rival, Sir Walter Raleigh, and that he was also trying to prove that he could outdo the university wits at their own game of verbal acrobatics.

A sense of style and elegance is the essence of this play, and the most suitable costume seems one which slightly exaggerates the fashions of the period (*c* 1580). A permanent set is needed that will support the mood of the play without obtruding on it.

After a long period of neglect, *Love's Labour's Lost* has risen both in critical and in theatrical opinion. From being regarded by such a critic as Hazlitt as prentice work of little intrinsic interest, and by many actors and producers as too full of elaborate word-play and topical allusions for any but a specialist audience, it is now widely accepted as belonging to much the same period as such other lyrical plays as *A Midsummer Night's Dream, Richard II* and *Romeo and Juliet.* Admittedly, it does contain numerous allusions to the intellectual quarrels of its own day, but this has not prevented the success of many recent productions, both amateur and professional. The play's wit is really independent of its original circumstances: bragging, affectation and the overturning of unrealistic plans are perennial targets of satire, and a modern audience can enjoy the absurdity of Armado and Holofernes without worrying whether Armado mocked Raleigh or Holofernes mocked the then famous scholar Gabriel Harvey. If, of course, the play is presented in a college where both performers and many of the audience are familiar with such questions, this will add another dimension of interest, but it is certainly not essential.

Regarded as a production, *Love's Labour's Lost* has two important advantages and one difficulty. The difficulty is that demand for stylized elegance in all the court characters which can be hard to find even in otherwise good performers. The two advantages are the abundance of good parts and the simplicity of the setting. There are no fewer than sixteen really attractive acting parts, and even Marcadé, not included in the sixteen, has one of the most dramatically effective entrances in Shakespeare. Moreover, five of these good parts are for women, an unusually high number. So this play may be more satisfactory to perform in than some of Shakespeare's more famous works. As the whole action occurs in 'The King of Navarre's Park', one set is enough, and the only technical problem here is to devise a satisfactory hiding-place for Berowne in Act I, scene 3, and it is easy enough to solve this.

Traditional stage setting

Setting

At the simplest, *Love's Labour's Lost* could be played with plain curtains at the back; a box-hedge or ornamental iron railings with a central entrance upstage; and a pavilion on each side, set below the hedge or railings. It would be both visually and practically helpful if the hedge or railings and the area behind could be raised by two or three steps. This would make for more effective centre entrances and would be useful for the pageant of the Nine Worthies in Act V. The pavilions could be light and easy to make: drapes on a frame, with decorative tops. They should be set against the wings, so that entrances and exits can be made through them. If more varied lighting effects are desired and practicable, a cyclorama could be used instead of curtains.

A more elaborate set could include a painted backcloth with trees, hills and perhaps buildings, separate cut-out trees, and at least one bigger and more ornate pavilion, from whose awning the court party could watch the pageant. Whatever set is chosen, we must remember the special qualities of the play. It has often been compared to a ballet, and a study of ballet sets can be rewarding.

We now come to the problem of the hiding places for the four lovers in IV. 3. One may say at the outset that this is a particularly 'balletic' scene, and that therefore we need not trouble about realistic probability. Shakespeare did not! He makes all four come to the same place in quick succession. Each in turn confides to the audience that he has broken his freshly made vow of three years' devotion to celibate study by falling in love at the first opportunity. Each hides on the appearance of his successor and hears *his* confession. Berowne, the first to arrive, comments on the others in turn. Conventions of timing, hiding and asides could hardly be pressed farther.

The King, Longaville and Dumain can easily hide in or behind the pavilions or behind the hedge. They must be visible to the audience at moments, while their invisibility to their fellows must keep its minimal credibility: that is all we need. Berowne's hiding-place is a little more difficult. Between Longaville's hiding and Dumain's entrance, Berowne says: 'Like a demi-god here sit

I in the sky.' This clearly implies he is looking down on the others from some markedly high place. In the simpler set, he could retire into the wings when he sees the King coming, climb a ladder set off-stage to a platform from which he could show his head and shoulders to the audience when necessary. On the more elaborate set with free-standing trees, a ladder could be set behind one of them. The branches of the tree could be so arranged that he would seem to be climbing it. If this device is used, the tree must be far enough downstage for Berowne to make his asides audible without shouting them blatantly across his unsuspecting companions.

Costume

There are three main types of costume required: for the courtiers, for the characters of lower rank, and for disguised characters, the Nine Worthies and 'Russians'.

To emphasize the balletic quality of the play, the courtiers could wear tights, tunics and short cloaks. The designer can ring all sorts of changes on this basic costume, colours being the most obvious. These, one feels, should be light but never harsh or strident. Pastel shades could be widely used. Different kinds of collar and sleeve, varied hats, cloak shapes and trimmings, garters, sashes and jewellery, will all add to the spectacle and help the audience to recognize the characters. Shoes can be decorated with rosettes or slashed into patterns. Gloves too can play a useful part, both decoratively and to emphasize gesture.

The ladies could wear a modified version of late Elizabethan costume. Its angularity could be exaggerated to suit the stylized quality of the production. Certainly these delightful and witty young ladies have a polished sharpness that goes well with an elegant angularity of dress.

Now to apply these generalizations to individual characters. The King of Navarre must have a royal dignity, yet he is also a comic, almost an absurd, figure. He not only shares the absurdity common to all four of the 'academicians' who break their vows almost as soon as they have made them, but he adds other touches of the ridiculous. He swears to avoid all women in total oblivion of the fact that diplomatic necessity no less than courtesy will

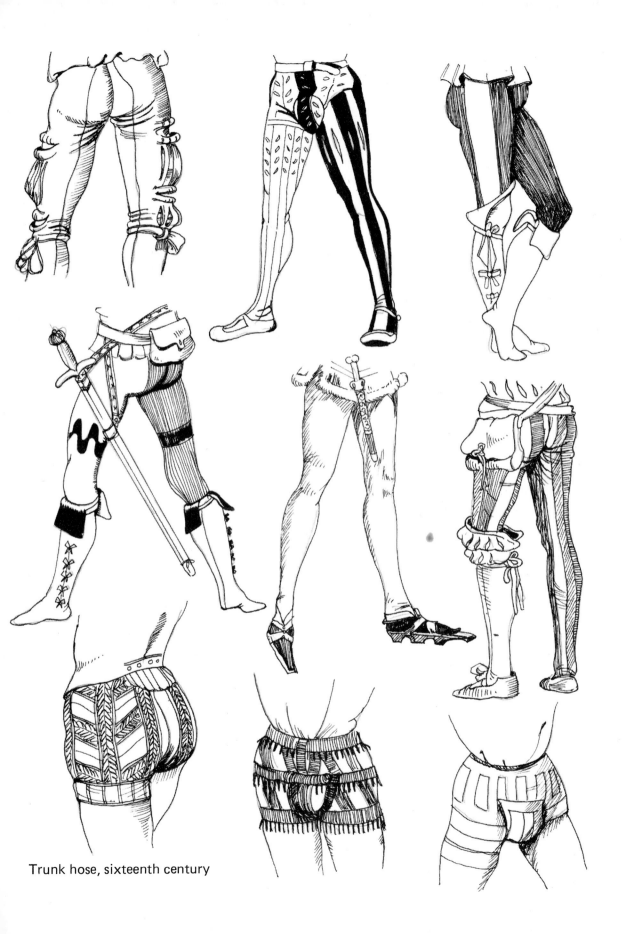

Trunk hose, sixteenth century

The King and Princess

force him to break his vow immediately by receiving the Princess. When this is pointed out to him, he exclaims in comic dismay, 'Why this was quite forgot!' (I. 1. 139).

Later, (V. 2. 534-537) he shares an inability to count with the fantastic Armado and the clown Costard. Gold and white might be his basic colours, and a gold chain could indicate his rank.

Whether or not we accept Dame Frances Yates's interesting theory of a connection between Berowne and the brilliant and ill-fated Giordano Bruno, Berowne is by far the liveliest and most individual of the quartet: red and gold would aptly symbolize his rich vitality. Stripes of blue and yellow and a high-crowned hat with feathers would emphasize Longaville's height. Green and violet could characterize the rather uncertain Dumain.

The Princess, like the King, needs some external sign of rank: her hat might suggest a diadem or coronet without too closely approaching it. The painting of Queen Elizabeth I standing on a map of Oxfordshire (in the National Portrait Gallery) could stimulate ideas, though it would need some lightening in quality to suit a young princess rather than a mature queen. The padded sleeves, for example, might be replaced either by closer-fitting or by loosely flowing ones. Each of the ladies might have the same basic colour as her lover or she might have a complementary colour. In either case, there would be both a visual and a psychological harmony. The ladies, too, need to change from their travelling clothes of Act II to the gorgeous costumes appropriate to the last act. For the hunting scene (IV. 1), they could easily wear a modified form of the travelling costume: a slight raising of the skirts to show leather boots, Robin Hood hats with feathers, plus their bows and belts with quivers attached. If the company had the resources to be lavish, they could have a completely different third set. Renaissance pictures of Diana and her attendants would help here.

Marcadé must wear complete black, relieved only by a white collar or ruff. As a traveller, he would naturally wear cloak and boots.

'Honey-tongued Boyet' seems definitely older than the four lovers, yet even more affected. His hat-feathers should be even more elaborately coloured and shaped; the toes of his shoes even more fantastically curled; his gloves longer, his ruff higher and more intricately patterned, his jewellery more ostentatious. Violets and silvers seem to fit both his greater age and his preciosity.

Armado is equally fantastic but in quite a different way. Some of the Second Folio directions refer to him specifically as 'a braggart'. We must remember this but not exaggerate it. Although his dramatic ancestry stretches back through the Commedia dell'Arte to the *miles gloriosus* (boastful soldier) of Roman comedy, Armado is a character in his own right. He is absurd but not contemptible. There is no suggestion of cowardice about him, as there is about many of his theatrical ancestors, and at the end he meets ridicule with dignity. His clothes must emphasize the soldier. Boots, large trunk hose, a high-crowned hat with prominent feathers, and a long, ostentatiously hilted sword, can help the required effect. He should be 'bearded like the Pard' in a noticeably aggressive style.

The text emphasizes the older meaning of 'Moth' ('small'; a variant of 'mote'), while his quick pertness suggest the modern meaning, though 'butterfly' would be more appropriate still. He has been dressed as a miniature of his master, and though Granville Barker condemns this as coarsening the humour, one can imagine its working well. Granville Barker's own suggestion that he should wear the King's livery – in this case, gold and white stripes – is also interesting and workable. Thirdly, his clothes might suggest a moth or butterfly. Whatever the details, smartness and airy quickness are the essentials.

One pictures Holofernes and Sir Nathaniel as similarly dressed, as the traditional link between teacher and priest remained strong. Both could wear black cassocks and academic gowns, but Holofernes should be more extravagant in every sense of the word. He should wear an obviously more expensive cloth; his linen must be more obtrusive and ornamental. He would, for instance, wear a ruff, whereas Nathaniel would wear clerical bands.

Costard, like Moth, might wear the King's livery: Armado, in his letter to the King, calls him 'the base minnow of *thy* (my italics) mirth'

Armado, Moth, Sir Nathaniel, Holofernes and Costard

(I. 1. 236) but 'clown', his description in the Dramatis Personae, and 'vassal', also in Armado's letter (I. 1. 241), both in this context mean 'rustic' or 'bumpkin', so we have no clear indication of his status. The producer seems free to present him as either a smartly liveried servant, which might explain his attraction for Jaquenetta, or as a plainly dressed countryman.

Jaquenetta herself should give an impression of slightly vulgar rural smartness. A yellow skirt, and a red bodice opening to show a laced blouse cut low is the sort of underbred lusciousness that would both respond to Costard and yet captivate the inflated pride of Armado. An effective change in her manner to her two admirers would be made if she tightened the laces of her blouse when talking to Armado, to give a less crudely bosomy display.

Having dealt with the costumes of the characters when they appear as their normal selves, we now come to their disguises: the Russian Mask of the four lovers, and the pageant of the Nine Worthies. Fortunately, we have contemporary accounts of Russian embassies to Queen Elizabeth's court, and Giles Fletcher's *Of the Russe Common Wealth* (1591) gave a detailed description of Russian life and customs.

A masking version of their dress could consist of shoulder capes over pearl-clasped robes, just short enough to show red leather boots with high heels. Each robe should be in the wearer's dominant colour, to help identification by the audience. Their masks should be fully moustached, whiskered and bearded.

Their attendant 'Blackamoors' could wear either white Moroccan robes or leopard skins. The costumes worn in the pageant of the Nine Worthies should contrast sharply both with the Russian disguises of the nobles and with the everyday wear of the performers. They must be much less elegant, much more homespun than the Russian disguises, yet much more colourful than their ordinary clothes. Everything should have an obviously homemade appearance. In detail, Costard as Pompey should wear breastplate, skirt with labels, helmet with horsehair plumes, buskins and leggings and a long cloak. If the producer accepts the interpretation that Berowne's 'You lie' implies that Costard trips and falls as he

enters, an excessively long cloak could supply the cause. He also needs a sword and shield, the shield bearing a leopard's —or, according to some experts — a lion's head, the traditional arms of Pompey. 'With libbard's head on knee' he may be interpreted literally, as the head was sometimes sometimes represented on the elbow or knee of garments. There is no reason why it should not appear in all three places: it might add to the absurdity.

Nathaniel, rather surprisingly cast as Alexander, would be rather similarly dressed, but his armour could be gold instead of silver, his cloak more heavily fringed, and his shield oval instead of oblong. Differentiating his arms presents a problem, as he too was traditionally associated with the lion, a fact that might decide the producer in favour of the leopard for Costard. Alexander's conventional weapon was the axe.

As Judas Maccabaeus, Holefernes could wear a blue helmet and breastplate with gold decorations, and a matching skirt over red hose and tunic. His weapon could either be an outsize hammer, in allusion to the probably false derivation of his surname, or with the curved sword Botticelli gave Judith, another heroic Hebrew. The lion was also associated with Hercules, but in the form of a complete skin, which Moth could wear over a short tunic. The contrast between his smallness and the legendary size and strength of Hercules is comic enough in itself.

Armado as Hector, perhaps the most convincing casting in the pageant, is yet another who needs classical armour and robes.

Lighting

This is very straightforward. As with every other aspect of this play, colourfulness, clarity and elegance are the essentials. There is the possibility of dimming or hardening the lighting when Marcadé brings the news of the King of France's death, but this should be treated with great discretion. The appearance of the black-clad messenger and the reactions of the other characters create a very powerful impact in themselves. A change of lighting, unless handled very tactfully, can seem merely hamfisted. This is probably something for the producer to experiment with before deciding.

The Masque style

The Tempest

The special qualities of the masque * were impressive scenery, elaborate machinery for spectacular effects, and emphasis on music and dancing. Originating in primitive rituals, it developed through folk mumming plays. During the sixteenth and seventeenth centuries, it rose socially, both on the Continent and in England, where it reached the height of fashion in the Jacobean and Caroline periods. In the latter, the spectacular and musical elements tended to swamp everything else. Ben Jonson's abandonment of the masque in 1634 marked the end of his long struggle to preserve dramatic and literary values against the influence of Inigo Jones, the great architect and stage-designer.

It is generally agreed that, of all Shakespeare's plays, *The Tempest* is the most deeply influenced by the masque style. Prospero's spirit-show to Ferdinand and Miranda (IV. 1) has many masque elements: classical goddesses, one descending from heaven 'in her car' (see page 66): a court performance. including a direct address to the royal bride and groom, wishing them a happy marriage; 'a graceful dance', and a vanishing. The rest of the play, too, has many masque features. It takes place on an enchanted island and its action is controlled throughout by a magician. Two major characters, Ariel and Caliban, are non-human, though in

* 'Mask' is the older and more scholarly spelling, but we will use 'masque' to avoid confusion.

opposite ways. Prospero seems to have an unlimited number of spirits at his command. He raises a storm and causes a shipwreck to bring his old enemies unharmed to his island and to keep them spellbound there. There is repeated emphasis on illusion. Being Shakespeare's, *The Tempest* is much more than a masque, but it does seem particularly suitable to produce in the masque style. This does, of course, demand a very well-equipped theatre with good facilities for flying scenery and performers. It also needs a fairly deep stage for the characteristic perspective effects of masque scenery, as well as to give room for the flying. A proscenium arch is helpful, as it emphasizes the essential picturesqueness of the style. An apron can be used but it not necessary. Lighting, sound effects and music also play a major part in this style, while scenery and costume call for imaginative design and skilful execution.

Before going any further, it is important to remember that using the masque style does not mean turning Prospero's island into a pantomime never-never land of pretty fairies and roistering knockabout comics, with everybody happy, forgiving or forgiven, and reconciled at the end. Though Prospero's magic is strong enough to control the evil during the play, it did not protect him against his brother's treachery. Antonio and Sebastian, Stephano and Trinculo, are ready to murder, even when the only certain prize is the apparently bare island. Caliban has a more acceptable motive — the recovery of his island, which presumably he gets when the mortals have gone — but, whatever his better qualities, he is brutally violent. Prospero is finally ready to forgive, but Antonio and Sebastian are unrepentant to the end. Prospero abjures his magic and returns to his dukedom, but there — 'Every third thought shall be my grave' (V. 1. 311) and drives home this sombre message in the Epilogue — 'And my ending is despair'. Of course, this is not the whole story, but it is a vital part and one that is too often neglected.

So far as the performers are concerned, *The Tempest* is both demanding and rewarding. The cast is large: there are eighteen clearly specified characters, human and non-human, plus an indefinite number of sailors, reapers, nymphs and spirits. The range of parts is exceptionally wide in every age, rank and nature. Prospero has been a favourite part with many actors, but there has been considerable controversy about him. Many Romantics and post-Romantics saw him as Shakespeare himself, the master magician displaying his art for the last time and bidding farewell to it. At the opposite extreme, Lytton Strachey found him a cantankerous old man, gratuitously offensive to everyone he met. [1] Another interpretation sees him as an early, almost prophetic, vision of colonialism, with Prospero dispossessing Caliban and then degrading him to justify exploiting his necessary labour. This may seem an unbalanced view, but the Footsbarn Company in Cornwall used it to excellent effect by presenting Prospero as a caricature of the British Raj. Jan Kott, in one of his most provocative essays, [2] emphasizes Prospero's despair and the frailty of his hope. No lack of food for thought here.

There are several other good parts for mature, even elderly, actors. Gonzalo is 'the good old lord'. As long as Antonio is clearly younger than Prospero, and Sebastian than Alonso, their ages may range from the forties to the sixties. In *The Tempest*, Shakespeare subordinated the parts to the whole with unusual strictness. The result is the most unified of his plays, but hardly the amplest in characterization. He gives his actors all they need, but they must be skilled enough to use it all. Gonzalo must combine genuine loyalty and

kindness with equally genuine muddleheadedness. Antonio must convey that special sort of shrewd realism limited by moral blindness that Shakespeare gives his Machiavellians. Sebastian must follow him, yet be a distinct personality; slower witted and less imaginative, though equally unscrupulous: a nastier and more formidable Roderigo to Antonio's more aristocratic Iago. Their relationship is broadly parodied by Stephano and Trinculo, who are as ambitious, unscrupulous and murderous as their social superiors. This must not be overlaid by excessive clowning. They are indeed buffoons, but sinister buffoons: one can visualize Coluche as Stephano.

Ferdinand and Miranda are comparatively straightforward. Ferdinand must justify Miranda's 'he's gentle and not fearful', remembering that this description probably included the meaning that Ferdinand was nobly born and so not easily frightened. The audience should be able to accept Miranda's age as fifteen (I. 2. 40-41 and 53) without straining credulity. Apart from her, the only speaking female characters are the goddesses in the spirit show; this being the play's one serious limitation in casting. Ariel has often been played by an actress, sometimes superbly, but sometimes with too much of the prettification we deplored earlier.

Caliban may be interpreted in many ways: as the victim of colonial exploitation; as an incarnation of the elements of earth and water; as an incarnation of the Id; of passion and instinct uncontrolled by reason; or as the 'savage and deformed slave' of the Folio. Whatever the interpretation, he must present a violent paradox: he responds to beauty with magnificent poetry; unlike Stephano and Trinculo, he is not distracted from the plot by the gaudy trumpery set to divert them. Yet he presents the image of the murder with peculiar brutality — 'paunch him with a stake' — he relishes the thought of raping Miranda, regretting only his failure. Above all, he mistakes Stephano for a god, though here, and in other ways, he learns wisdom. Ariel is more consistent, dominated by his desire for pure freedom.

If the demands, human and material, we have listed seem somewhat daunting, it is encouraging to remember that many of them may be qualified in various ways, while others are peculiar to this style of production, and can be avoided by using a different presentation. Doubling and trebling of roles make the play possible for a comparatively small company. Given good acting, a performance in front of plain curtains, with appropriate music and the simplest sound and lighting effects, can produce a very fine *Tempest* indeed. I have seen the opening scene most vividly portrayed on a bare platform, with the pitching and tossing of the ship most giddily projected by the mere swaying of the actors' bodies. Why then the more elaborate production I am about to describe? Simply that it is one of the many production styles legitimately applicable to Shakespeare; that it is particularly suited to this play; and that it can bring out some of *The Tempest's* special qualities.

Setting

The action of *The Tempest* takes place in three basic settings: the ship's deck for the opening storm scene; in or near Prospero's cell; unspecified parts of the island.

Though the effects of the storm can be very powerfully conveyed by the actors themselves, our production style calls for something much more spectacular. A section of the ship's deck can be mounted on a central roller, below the stage, so that it can be swung from side to side, either mechanically or by man power. The movement must have a natural irregularity, and it must be well supported by lighting and sound effects, to simulate flashes of lightning, peals of thunder and the roaring of wind. A receding series of wings, showing characteristic features of the island — hills, streams and thickets — can occasionally be glimpsed through the confusion of the storm.

At the end of scene 1, the rocking deck will return to a level with the rest of the deck, and be fastened in place. The mast, rigging and whatever other nautical paraphernalia with which the producer has dressed the set, can be struck either behind a drop-curtain or under cover of the darkness into which the storm can naturally develop. We can then progress easily into the comparative calm of Prospero's cell, disturbed only by the more distant sound of the storm in

the beginning. The cell would descend from the flies, and could take the form of a cave mouth, opening to show the traditional equipment of a white magician: a table or tables strewn with large volumes, mathematical and musical instruments, glass vessels of varied shapes, and scrolls; perhaps a cabbalistic Tree of Life, big enough for some of the signs to be recognized in the audience. Most of these would have to be fixed firmly to keep their places when the cell is raised and lowered, but some of the fastenings should be arranged so that Prospero could pick up and handle them. Behind the cell, a sky backcloth would be visible.

For the unspecified parts of the island, the cell would be flown and the producer would have the whole stage at his disposal. In Act II, scene 1, Shakespeare emphasizes that the good and the bad characters see the island and their own garments differently (49-66). The producer might support this visually by having the wings light on one side, sombre on the other. He could achieve further variations and subtleties by using *periaktoi* instead of ordinary flats. In any case, the receding wings should give the perspective effect typical of this theatrical style.

Costume

Until the last scene, Prospero's basic costume could be a plain but rich doublet — say, purple with gold buttons and trimmings — worn over loose breeches of the same colour, violet stockings and purple shoes. When he is acting specifically as a magician, he could wear a voluminous, ankle-length cloak, fastened at the shoulders, and big enough to be draped over one arm or shoulder. It could have a hood attached, and it should be coloured so as to blend easily into the background when he is supposed to be invisible. The traditional wands of white magicians were of ash, hazel or oak, tipped with metal.

When, in the final scene, he appears as 'absolute Milan', he could project the transformation by wearing a long robe of gold and black brocade, open from the waist to show a gold and crimson lining. He could wear double sleeves, the outer loose and matching the cloak; the inner, close-fitting, of gold and crimson with lace cuffs. He

Prospero and Miranda with Ferdinand in front of Prospero's cell

could also wear a broad chain of gold and jewels from shoulder, resting on an ermine background. A high black velvet hat bound with a gold chain would suggest his ducal coronet, while an ivory and gold sceptre would symbolize the change from magician to earthly ruler.

Whatever particular ornaments Antonio may wear, the prevailing impression should be a sickly green with gold jewels and braid, thus combining symbols of rank with those of treachery and jealousy, and also carrying out Shakespeare's own suggestion that the clothes of the evil characters looked stained by the storm. In view of his attempt at murder, a conspicuously jewelled sword-belt and basket-hilted rapier would suit him well. Sebastian, who is so much Antonio's shadow, could be similarly dressed in parti-coloured doublet and cloak of green and yellow to indicate his rather inchoate nature.

Alonso, King of Naples, stands between the definitely good and the definitely evil characters. His enmity to Prospero had been open, not treacherous. His grief for his apparently lost son is genuine. He wins sympathy as the intended victim of his brother and his supposed ally. Finally, he repents sincerely of his part in Prospero's wrongs. His clothes can reflect this by being less stained than Antonio's and Sebastian's, though not as fresh as Gonzalo's. Their general style should be similar to Prospero's as Duke, but differing in colour, details and ornament.

Gonzalo, whose goodness is emphasized from the beginning, says that his garments seem 'rather new-dy'd, than stain'd with salt water'. Grey and blue seem suited both to his age and his character: a grey, blue-lined cloak over grey doublet and hose, trimmed with silver. The canions could be dark blue, worn with grey netherstocks and black shoes with silver buckles.

Adrian and Francisco will vary according to the ages of their actors. If young, they would be elegant, though comparatively unobtrusive courtiers with short cloaks, doublets and hose; if older, they would dress more like Gonzalo.

As *The Tempest* was almost certainly performed as part of the festivities celebrating the betrothal of King James the first's enchanting daughter, Princess Elizabeth, to Frederick, the Elector Palatine, it seems suitable to take portraits of Frederick and Elizabeth as models for Ferdinand and Miranda. This would give him a wide-brimmed, high-crowned hat with a plume in front; a ruff with intricate lace decorations; a short cloak to be draped over the arm, worn over a jewelled doublet with short jewelled skirt; baggy slops reaching almost to the knees; jewelled garters, and shoes with flower pompons. He also wears a miniature, or the jewel of an order, hanging round his neck.

As Prospero tells us (I. 2. 164) that Gonzalo had provided them with 'Rich garments, linens, stuffs, 'Miranda can dress more elaborately than we might otherwise suppose a marooned princess. Princess Elizabeth wore a hat with the brim turned back to show rich jewelling; an open ruff with intricate lace decorations; a patterned fichu over a low bodice, which is decorated with a string of pearls and rosettes down the centre; finally, a round farthingale with brocaded skirt. If this seems too elaborate for the early scenes, she could wear a simplified version for them.

Trinculo would wear the grey-green motley coat of his profession, with belt and pouch; Stephano, a cloak, doublet and hose in the green and gold livery of his master.

The sailors would wear the normal dress of their trade. The Captain could wear the plainer sort of gentleman's clothing. His doublet and hose might be in the royal livery, and he would wear a long seacloak. So would the Boatswain, whose clothes would resemble the ordinary sailors' but show superiority in style and material. He must have a whistle on a chain or cord.

We now come to the varied non-human characters. Caliban's gabardine could have a surface like fish scales, to justify Trinculo's 'What have we hear? a man or a fish?' There might be padding to suggest deformity. His tunic could be a pale greyish white, suggesting the underbelly of a fish. His arms and legs could protrude in scaly sleeves and stockings. Webbed feet are a possible finishing touch.

A very simple costume, such as black tights and a plain white shirt could express Ariel's essential independence and lightness better than wings and gauze.

The spirits who act in Prospero's entertainment for Ferdinand and Miranda would certainly wear

Stephano Caliban and Trinculo

Sailors

the traditional costumes of their roles. Iris would wear a long, draped tunic, gold sandals and a bandeau, and she would carry a long sceptre or a corn-sheaf. Ceres's robe would be long, perhaps corn coloured; she would have a veil on the back of her head, and be crowned with ears of corn. Juno would also carry a long sceptre, a similar veil, a diadem, and a peacock robe over a gold chiton. The nymphs would wear chitons, moderately embroidered at neck, wrist and hem, and they could be bare legged.

The reapers would wear smocks over gaitered leggings and would carry reaping hooks.

Lighting

Two main types of lighting are needed: one to give storm effects; straightforward lighting for the rest. Within these two categories, there is scope for wide variations that can greatly enhance the dramatic impact.

The most violent storm effects are needed in the first scene, where the lightning flashes, carefully co-ordinated with the sounds of thunder, roaring wind and breaking waves, are vital to the scene. The same effects, slightly milder, should continue into the beginning of I. 2, until Prospero removes his magic cloak (I. 2. 24-25), when the magically engendered storm would naturally cease. At the beginning of II. 2, there should be thunderous, overcast sky. It would be well within the masque tradition to have cut-out clouds moving across in front of the backcloth, but this would still need help from the lighting. Then there must be some thunder and lightning to support Trinculo's 'Alas, the storm is come again!' This should be less violent than the storm in I. 1, but enough to justify Trinculo's acquainting himself with so strange a bedfellow as Caliban. In III. 3, the thunder and lightning are magically produced, and can therefore strike suddenly without natural preparation. Precise timing is needed after line 51: the darkness that follows a vivid flash of lightning being a useful cover for the 'quaint device' that makes the banquet vanish.

The rest of the lighting also calls for considerable variety. After the storm ceases in the early part of I.2, the lighting should convey calm, with concentration on the area in front of Prospero's cell. Act II, scene 2 needs full lighting. It would be an interesting experiment, though difficult to work out in detail, to emphasize the difference between the good and the evil characters already marked by their contrasted responses to the island and the condition of their own garments, by lighting them differently. In II. 2, after the storm dies away, the lighting could change gradually from dullness to brightness. III. 1 requires full lighting; III. 2, a concentration of light downstage. Act III, scene 3 should start full and dim when the 'solemn and strange music' starts. Moving spots should focus on the spirits and the banquet, staying on the latter when the spirits disappear. After the banquet disappears, the spots should stay on the royal party. Full lighting should come up again after the spirits' exit. Act IV, scene 1 should start with full lighting; dim for the spirits' exit; then focus on Prospero. The last scene should certainly have full lighting, both to make a large area of the stage fully visible, and to give visual support to the dramatic clarification. Dimming towards the end could underline the resigned melancholy of Prospero's last speeches.

Sound effects

These can be divided into three groups: music supposed to be played on stage; off-stage music; and other sounds.

The first are all clearly indicated in the text, and the producer's only problem is whether his actors can actually play the required instruments or will have to mime to music produced off-stage. Miming demands very careful rehearsal to avoid absurd mistakes. The actor's movements must be co-ordinated precisely with the music, which means either that actor and musician must see each other or that the actor can see a signal invisible to the audience. Furthermore, the actor's hands must make the right movements for the sounds he is supposed to produce. The only time I had to mime playing the piano in my acting career, I was lucky in that my wife, a professional pianist, told me exactly where my hands should be at each moment, and how my body should move. The second, or atmospheric, kind of music is a highly individual matter, which the producer must decide for himself. Discreetly used, off-stage music can help greatly, but one must always remember the awful examples of seventeenth and eighteenth century adaptations of Shakespeare to semi-opera.

The other sound effects are also clearly shown in the text; the most important are the storm effects already mentioned in connection with lightning. There are various ways of producing these, from the traditional thundersheet to a recording, which nowadays is probably the best.

Special effects

Apart from the sea storm, the most important special effects are those connected with the mysterious banquet in Act III, scene 3, and with Prospero's spirit show in Act IV, scene 1. As the 'strange Shapes' bring in the banquet already set,

the goblets, bowls of fruit and sweetmeats ('banquet' then meant 'dessert') can be fixed to the table-top. This can swivel on a pivot, operated either by Ariel or off stage, in the momentary darkness after the flash of lightning. When the audience can see again, an empty table will meet their eyes.

The most spectacular effect in Prospero's entertainment for Ferdinand and Miranda is the descent of Juno 'in her car'. The appearance of a *deus* — or *dea* — ex *machina* was a characteristic masque device. Contemporary illustrations often show the car as more like an elaborately decorated boat then a wheeled vehicle. It was sometimes large enough to carry attendants as well as the principal god or goddess. For this scene, it could be drawn by peacocks, the birds traditionally associated with Juno. The whole equipage would rest on canvas clouds, while other clouds hid the controlling wires.

A modern dress production

Romeo and Juliet

It would certainly seem illogical not to include one modern-dress production in our variety of styles, and of all Shakespeare's plays, *Romeo and Juliet* appears the most obvious candidate. Over the last fifteen to twenty years, I have certainly found it has the greatest, the most immediate appeal to teenagers. This popularity, of course, is nothing new but its special impact on the modern teenager suggests it would be even more effective if its costumes emphasized the basic themes that are probably the secret of its appeal: young love thwarted by parental attitudes and destroyed by inherited feuds.

The main problem so far as the company is concerned is to find enough young performers who can combine a vigorous, contemporary approach with effective speaking of their words. Fortunately there are plenty of young players who can speak the verse convincingly and make it express the characters and their emotions. There should be even less difficulty in finding competent performers for the older parts. A difference in style might even help to establish the generation gap without destroying the essential unity of the production.

As always in a modern-dress production of Shakespeare, there are some anachronisms. Mechanically, the most obvious is the sword-fighting. Socially and psychologically, the main problems are the bloody vendetta between two aristocratic families and the status of parental authority, claimed by Capulet and to some extent admitted, though rebelled against, by Juliet.

These problems can all be solved by giving the play a south-European or Latin American setting. This can, in fact, underline the generation gap by presenting the younger characters as belonging to the present, while their elders still cling to traditions that have long been abandoned in northern Europe and North America. Thus Juliet is modern enough to defy her parents in deed, but sufficiently conditioned by her upbringing to do so by stealth rather than open defiance. The older Capulets and Montagues can combine modern dress with a somewhat Mafia-like feuding.

This setting will solve the problem of the fights too. Rapiers are obviously out. Even if Romeo, Mercutio, Tybalt, Paris and Benvolio were all active members of their university fencing club, they could not all, with any plausibility, carry swords with them at the appropriate moments. Knives go much more easily with modern teenage dress, but in northern Europe and North America it is rare to find upper-class youths carrying them. This particular class barrier does not seem to operate, at any rate so strongly, in, for example, Sicily or the Argentine. So the sword fights can easily be turned to knife fights.

Other problems remain, whatever setting we choose, as Sir Edmund Chambers pointed out in

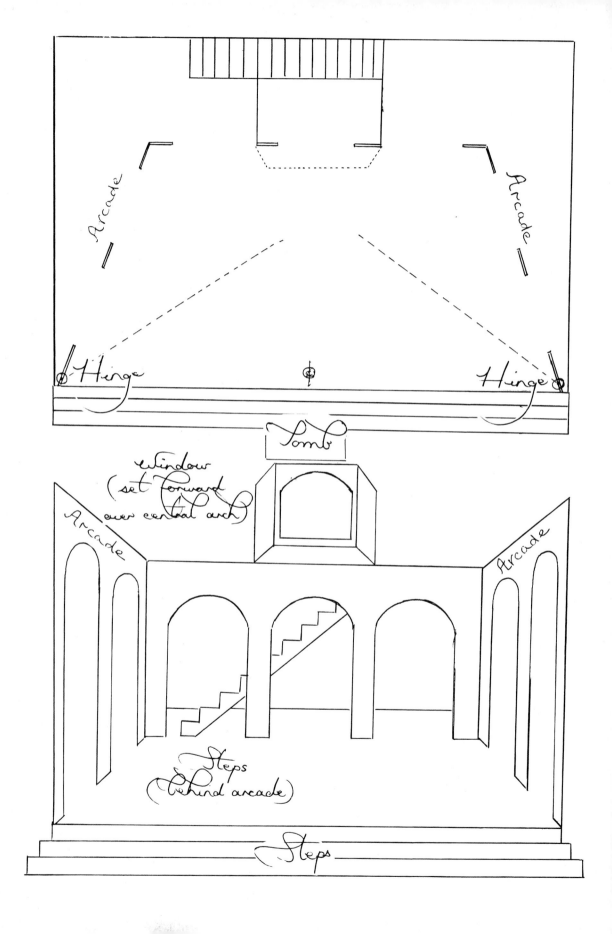

Arcade

Arcade

Hinge

Hinge

Tomb

Window
(set forward
over central arch)

Arcade

Arcade

Steps
(behind arcade)

Steps

his classic *The Elizabethan Stage* (vol III, pp 51, 83-84 and 94-95). There is the nature of the wall over which Romeo has to leap (II. 1); the question of whether we are inside or outside Friar Laurence's cell in III. 3; and, most of all, the questions about Juliet's bedroom — whether the audience see the inside or the outside in III. 5, and whether it is on the same level in IV. 3, and in IV. 5. One hardly notices these points when reading the play, and a good production makes them equally unobtrusive, but only at the cost of careful planning.

Setting

Picture an acting area on three levels. At floor-level, nearest to the audience, is a semi-circular space with a low tomb-like oblong in the centre, on which Juliet will lie in Act V. A few shallow steps lead up to the main stage, which has arcades at the back and on both sides. The side arcades are hinged downstage and mounted on rollers, so that they can be swung forward to form the walls and gates of the Capulet vault in the last scene. One of the side arches can be the entrance to Friar Laurence's cell, and one on the other side the opening of the Apothecary's stall in Mantua. Steps go up the front of the back wall, behind the arcade, so that they remain unobtrusive when not in use. There is space left and right of the side-walls for characters to enter, lurk, and for Romeo to climb into the Capulet garden.

The third level, reached either by the steps up the back wall or by steps backstage or in the wings, will have a balcony set over the central arch of the upstage arcade, which will project forward from the general line of the arches. Juliet's bed will also be set on this uppermost level, either R or L centre.

This is the basic plan. Much of the atmosphere of the production will depend on its detailed execution. The shape and decoration of the arches will direct the audience's imagination to Italy or Latin America. If the producer wants the Italian effect, almost any paintings or photographs of Verona itself or any other Italian town will suggest appropriate details. Similarly, pictures of several South American and Mexican towns will give details for the alternative. The producer will have to decide how much modernity he wants in the actual setting. He can leave an untouched Renaissance effect, as another reinforcement of the generation gap. He can add easily removable signs to some of the arcades, suggesting modern shops and boutiques. Or he can use wholly modern architecture, while keeping to the basic plan.

The second or main stage will represent an unspecified town square or street, and so will serve for all the exterior scenes in Verona and the one in Mantua. Furnished with tables and chairs, and appropriately lit, it will represent the main hall of the Capulets' house for the party scene (I. 5), where torches and cressets on stage will assist the ordinary stage lighting. The main stage can also represent other rooms of the Capulets, except for those scenes specifically set in Juliet's bedroom.

For the Balcony scene (II. 2) the main stage can represent the Capulet garden (the normal meaning of 'orchard' in Shakespeare's time). In Act II, scene 1, Romeo can enter at the corner of the steps leading from the main stage to the lower level, hide behind the outside walls of the main stage during Mercutio's mocking conversation with Benvolio, and climb this outer wall — on which, of course, proper hand and foot-holds must have been prepared — and climb or jump down on to the main stage for II.2.

The scenes connected with Friar Laurence's cell can be located in and near one of the downstage arches, which can be clearly identified by a crucifix over the top. The Apothecary's shop (V. 1) can also be set in one of the arches. If one of the upstage arches is used, the shop must be dressed with some, at least, of what Romeo describes in V. 1. 42-48. If an inside-arch is used, Romeo's speech can be taken to set the scene sufficiently.

As we mentioned above, there are problems concerning one of the scenes located in or near Friar Laurence's cell. Most of these scenes can be placed quite naturally just outside the entrance. The problem lies in Act III, scene 3. The first part is easy enough. Friar Laurence has obviously just heard the Prince's sentence of banishment on Romeo, so he would naturally approach his cell from outside, and, after looking round to make sure the coast was clear, he would summon Romeo, and their conversation too would take place just outside the cell. The problem, such as it is, arises when repeated knocking announces the Nurse's arrival. How are we to imagine her approach to the cell? If the same as Friar Laurence's, there would be no need for her to knock: she would see Romeo, and everybody, actors and audience alike, would see her at once. The simplest solution is to assume that the cell has a second entrance offstage and that the Nurse is knocking on its door. The Friar can then enter his cell as he is saying lines 75-79, so that the audience can only hear him during the last two or three lines, and then return with the Nurse. This is open to some questions and objections that would be hard to answer logically; fortunately, they are very unlikely to arise in the audience's mind. This basic plan, though in different settings, has often been used, and I have never known it to disturb anybody's response to the scene. Well directed lighting can focus attention of the part of the cell immediately outside the cell, and so prevent the feeling that it is all too public.

Apart from the Balcony scene, the highest level can be used for III. 2 and will certainly be used for the lovers' parting (III. 5). One problem here is the precise manner of Romeo's departure. Several references have already been made to a rope ladder for Romeo's ascent to Juliet's room and we actually see it when the Nurse brings the disastrous news of Tybalt's death. Some Romeos actually descend by this in full view of the audience. Some sling it over a back or side wall, thus suggesting they use it, while actually using steps out of the audience's sight. Others athletically leap from the balcony — always rather alarming. No Romeo can give his best with a sprained ankle. Others, taking the rope-ladder to have been sufficiently established by the dialogue, come down by a staircase. Our setting allows a free choice. A good deal will depend on the Romeo: on his agility and nerve. If both actor and producer are satisfied that the descent can be made by the rope ladder without danger of an unwanted comic effect, it must be secured firmly before the scene begins, so that there is no awkward hiatus to break the emotional impact of the scene, and whatever parts of the scenery have to take the strain must be adequately reinforced.

The three levels will also help to solve the problems of scenes 3, 4 and 5 of Act IV. At the end of scene 3, Juliet drinks the potion and collapses on her bed. Scene 4 begins with all the bustle of preparation for her wedding with Count Paris. This will naturally take place on the main stage, with plenty of movement from and into the various arches, which here represent entrances to different rooms in the Capulet house. Scene 5 can follow without a break. Capulet orders the Nurse to waken Juliet — 'Make haste, I say'. She goes immediately up the stairs, calling on her way. There are two or three places in her speech beginning, 'Mistress! What, mistress!' where she can look at the drugged Juliet before she feels alarm. The Producer must decide the exact entrances and positions of the Capulets, Paris and Friar Laurence. To avoid crowding the stairs, much of which are hidden by the arches, he might bring some of them on from the wings on the higher level. Lady Capulet, at least, would quite naturally enter on that level, as if from another bedroom. The Friar and Count Paris would be more likely to enter on the main stage, as if from the house's main gate. Capulet could use either level. After the general exit of the mourners (5. 95), the Nurse comes down the stairs and leaves by one of the upstage exits after her two lines to the musicians. They can then play the rest of the scene, with its total change of mood, well downstage.

The special advantage of this set for the last scene is that Romeo and Juliet can play their death scenes right downstage, in the closest contact with the audience. The different levels also corroborate the references to a vault and to descending into the tomb.

Under cover of darkness, Juliet will take her place on the tomb-like platform on the lowest level, and the side arches will have been swung or rolled forward to join in forming a wall across the lower part of the main stage. One of the arches near the centre will have a permanent 'iron' door, or the two that meet in the centre could join in such a way as to form a large double door. The others, open for the rest of the play, could have 'iron' grilles hung from the inside so as to present a physical barrier to the vault while not entirely blocking the audience's view. Entrances may be either from the highest level or from the main stage. The dramatic silhouette against the night sky would make the highest entrance more suitable for Romeo. The general crowding in at the end would need all the entrances. The producer will have some interesting decisions to make about the rest. The fight between Romeo and Paris will doubtless use all levels, though most will be at the top, for the sake of visibility, but Romeo must not have to carry the body of Paris too far into the tomb: he will need all his reserves of acting power and breath for his long and beautiful last speech. After the death of Juliet, as the stage fills with Watch, Capulets and Montagues, Friar Laurence, and finally the Prince and his train, the whole acting area will be needed, with the Prince and the finally reconciled families round the tomb of the lovers, and the rest grouped to fill the stage from the lowest level to those silhouetted against the sky. Either a slow fade-out on this tableau, or a solemn procession off — or, indeed, a combination of the two — would express the 'glooming peace' that ends the play after the tragic climax of the lovers' deaths.

Costume

So far as clothing is concerned, the speed with which teenage fashions change make it useless to prescribe details. For these, the producer must simply go by what he sees in the streets, discos and teenage boutiques. There are, however, some essential principles. Romeo and his friends would dress in the height, not the depth, of whatever may be the contemporary fashion at the time of production. Their clothes must look expensive: jet set, not drop out. A *possible* exception is Mercutio. The producer may consider his mockery of Tybalt's devotion to the latest style in fencing, his characteristic mixture of poetry and bawdry, and his inner detachment both from love and from the Montague-Capulet vendetta — 'A plague a' both your houses!' — suggest his dress should contrast with that of the other young men. He could have a touch of the contemporary equivalent of the hippie style.

Should the two sides be distinguished in any

way by their dress? A visible difference could simplify matters for the audience, and, if there was a recognizible style-division current among teenagers at the time of production, this might be used. In such a case, though, the producer would have to consider whether this might set off an irrelevant and even dangerous response in the audience. Alternatively, the producer might differentiate the two parties by some basic colour or colours, without, of course, approaching any hint of a uniform. He might, for example, take Tybalt, the most aggressive of the Capulets, and use the cat-reference to him as a basis for associating the Capulets with suede or even velvet, if it happened to be fashionable, and with tawny silks. Similarly, he could take Juliet's famous line

> That which we call a rose
> By any other name would smell as sweet.

as a hint, and dress Romeo and his friends in rose-coloured silks with green waistcoats or jackets of leather.

The masks worn by Romeo and the other gate-crashers at the Capulet party would be most effective if they related to something highly topical, so that also would be a matter of choosing at the time.

The servants who brawl in the first scene could be liveried footmen. The indoor servants in the party scene would dress as modern waiters and waitresses. The musicians in IV. 5. should be a pop group of the more fantastically dressed sort, to help the change of mood here.

The older Montagues and Capulets and the Prince would all wear suits subdued in colour but clearly giving the impression of first-class tailoring. Capulet and the older male guests should, I think, wear white tie and tails at the party, to mark the generation gap. When the older characters appear in the final scene, they have all been summoned hastily from their beds. Overcoats, hats and scarves would be in order. If they can give the effect of haste without losing dignity, it would be excellent. A skilful adjustment of the scarf can sometimes produce the required effect.

Modern dress makes it harder to mark the Prince's rank, but he could wear a chain of office, like a mayor's, and he could have a regular guard uniformed like carabinieri or some equivalent military or para-military police.

Friar Laurence would wear a Franciscan habit: a long, loose robe, bound at the waist with a cord, and a matching chaperon. Originally an indeterminate grey, it is now brown.

Almost any modern clothing would do for the Apothecary, as long as it was shabby enough. He might wear a once-decent suit worn threadbare or he might look a conscious member of the alternative society.

Juliet's clothes, like those of her male contemporaries, would depend on the fashion at the time of production, though I think her father would insist on her wearing a dress for the party. When the Nurse finds her apparently dead in her room she exclaims, 'What, dress'd and in your clothes,' — which, in modern dress, clearly implies a wedding-dress for this and her last scene.

Like their husbands', Lady Capulet's and Lady Montague's clothes would suggest wealth rather than ostentation, though Lady Capulet's youth — she cannot be more than thirty (I. 3. 72-74) — would make her noticeably smarter.

A rather traditional nurse's uniform would be in order here: ankle-length black dress with white collar and cuffs and a white wimple. The formal effect of this should be modified by a distinctively though not exaggeratedly casual, even untidy manner of wearing it. The collar could be open; the wimple not too scrupulously starched; the black stockings could sag a little over the ankles.

Lighting

Apart from its essential job of letting the audience see clearly what is happening, lighting in *Romeo and Juliet* has two important functions: to indicate different times of day and night, and to reinforce the mood of each scene. The two functions often overlap. For example, Act III, scene 1 is the turning point of the play. Up till then, despite every obstacle, all has gone well for the lovers. After, despite moments of ecstatic happiness, things go against them until they are both dead. The essential cause of this change is Romeo's killing of Tybalt, which leads to his banishment with all its consequences. His killing of Tybalt is

the direct result of Tybalt's killing of Mercutio, and the opening lines of the scene explicitly connect this fatal quarrel with the atmosphere of the day:

> *Benvolio* I pray thee, good Mercutio, let's retire.
> The day is hot, the Capulets abroad,
> And if we meet we shall not scape a brawl.
> For now, these hot days, is the mad blood stirring.

This clearly demands lighting that is hot and bright, expressing the destructive power, not the creativity, of the sun: the same sort of inhuman brightness that led Meursault to shoot the nameless Arab in Camus's *The Outsider*.

This peculiar light should reach its greatest intensity in this scene but it should also be present in the brawl in I. 1. Equal warmth and brightness but less harshness should be present in the other outdoor daytime scenes.

Two scenes, one vitally important, take place in the dawn. Friar Laurence brings his herbs home in 'grey-ey'd morn' (II. 3); the night sky is just streaked and 'jocund day, Stands tiptoe on the misty mountain tops' when the lovers part after their wedding night (III.5). Care and subtlety are needed to differentiate between these two.

Most of the interiors vary only in the area lighted and in the intensity of lighting. The party scene must give a bright and festive impression, though there may be patches of darkness, of privacy, into which groups and lovers can disappear. In other interiors, such as Juliet's bedroom, lighting would be more concentrated. The final scene demands both varied and tactful lighting, which shows action, assists atomosphere, indicates passage of time, but does not call attention to itself. The scene is partly exterior, showing the graveyard; partly interior, showing the Capulet vault. It begins in the dead of night and ends in an overcast morning. So the producer can begin with spots following the torches of the individual visitors to the tomb; bring up more lighting on the tomb once Romeo has entered the vault, and gradually bring up the background lighting as the stage crowds.

> A glooming peace this morning with it brings;
> The sun for sorrow will not show his head.

Ancient Rome seen through Renaissance eyes

Julius Caesar

As mentioned in the Introduction, there are at least three fairly obvious ways of producing *Julius Caesar*, each with special advantages and drawbacks.

Roman   Most obvious of all is to produce it in Roman costume in a Roman setting. This has the advantage of historical accuracy and of fitting in with the vivid, if not always quite accurate picture most of us have of ancient Rome. But it involves anachronisms which seem worse in discussion than in performance, and this style has long been the most popular for *Julius Caesar*.

Elizabethan   Anachronisms can be avoided by an Elizabethan style: doublets and late sixteenth century hats will be perfectly in keeping with the carpenter's leather apron and rule. Interesting though this might be as an experiment, the practical disadvantages would be severe. The initial shock to the audience's expectations would be hard to overcome, and there would be no counter-balancing gain in immediacy.

Modern dress   Immediacy, of course, is the great advantage of the third way: a production in modern dress. Political conspiracies, assassinations and *coups d'etat* are all too common in our own world. Caesar in a fascist-type uniform and other modern military uniforms for the battle scenes are easy enough to accept. The setting could suggest many contemporary cities, Rome itself, Prague, Buda-pest or the capital of some Third World state. Once again however there are difficulties, both in detail and in motivation. Antony stripped for the Lupercal might find a convenient parallel in some Third World country, but would be hard to accept in any modern European setting. Harder still are the suicides at the end: falling on one's sword seems extraordinarily clumsy and even absurd for an officer with a pistol.

Apart from technical problems, there are serious difficulties in political motivation. If Caesar is presented as a modern dictator, he is usually fascist or semi-fascist in style. His pomposity, his boastfulness, his superstition, his playing to the gallery, the contrast between his self-proclaimed constancy and his actual malleability, and his retinue of often hostile flatterers — all these are typical enough of his would-be successor, Mussolini. The problem lies in the opposition. If Caesar is a fascist, the conspirators must be Com-munists or democratic socialists or liberal demo-crats. But any interpretation in terms of class warfare is completely at odds with Shakespeare's text. The conspirators are made up of 'many of the best respect in Rome', that is of nobles. The *idea* of Rome and the traditional hatred of the name of 'king' are clearly emotional stimulants of great power, certainly to Brutus, perhaps to Shakespeare also; but their meaning is never made precise. True, even his enemy Mark Antony ascribes concern for 'the common good of all' to Brutus, and he himself, in his speech after the assassination (III. 2) appeals to the people's love of freedom. But the freedom seems curiously dis-embodied. The Roman people are portrayed as fickle, gullible and violent. Flavius and Marullus, the first opponents of Caesar that we meet, rate them angrily and speak of 'their basest metal', and this sets the tone. With one exception, they are there merely to be manipulated and cheated, or to lynch the wrong man, and that exception occurs off-stage, when, as Casca reports (I.2) their oppo-sition to kingship is strong enough to thwart Caesar. Even here it is noteworthy that Casca — the conspirator who struck the first blow — speaks of the crowd with the utmost contempt and seems chiefly impressed by their bad breath. Thus, while it is possible to interpret Brutus as the perennial high-minded but politically inept idealist, this conspiracy is intractable to a contemporary political interpretation.

So what do we do? We have looked at three pro-duction styles, found virtues but also difficulties in all. There remains a fourth possibility: what one may call the Renaissance style.

Renaissance style This designates the mixture of fifteenth to seventeenth century with classical style used by so many painters of the period. Granville-Barker takes as an example Paul Veronese's 'Alexander and the Wife and Daughter of Darius' in the National Gallery, but there are many other examples. For the men, a vaguely classical breastplate and sandals combine with Elizabethan doublet and hose. The breastplate is moulded to the body in a way that obviously appealed strongly to the Renaissance visual imagi-nation. This style, paradoxically both anachronistic and historically apposite, solves all the problems we have been discussing. Hats, doublets and leather aprons will all be in place, yet our pictures of Rome — both imaginery and imaginative — will be satisfied. Motives will present no problem, for the conspirators, when they are not moved by obvious and easily comprehensible 'envy of great Caesar', will have the powerful yet dis-

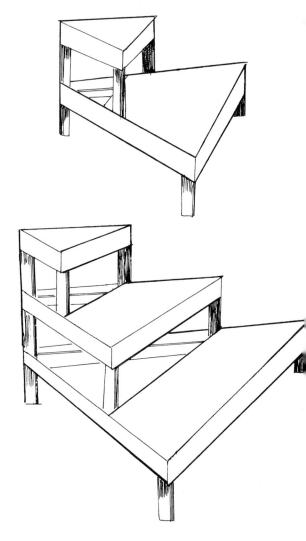

embodied image of Rome which so stirred the minds of Renaissance men.

This then is the style I shall adopt for *Julius Caesar*, without thereby denying the validity of any other style. In addition to the advantages, already mentioned, it gives plenty of opportunity for rich scenic effects, and it has moreover a long stage history. The earlist illustrations we have of any play by Shakespeare, the Longleat drawing of 'Titus Andronicus' attributed to Henry Peacham and endorsed 1595, shows a fundamentally similar mixture, though with a greater stress on the Eliza-bethan than would be easy to accept today. The tradition persisted, with variations, until the Romantic movement brought a desire for historical accuracy.

Setting

The essential is a backcloth painted with the traditional symbols of classical Rome: colonnades, Roman arches, perhaps specific Roman buildings. As a certain kind of anachronism is an intrinsic part of this style, it is irrelevant that this is the Rome of Augustus, even of the Antonines, rather than the Rome of Julius Caesar. It is the *idea* of Rome rather than any specific Rome that we wish to project. Pompey's statue, at the foot of which Caesar fell, may be a real statue, an item on the painted backcloth, or it may be left to the audience's imagination. If it is present from the beginning of the performance, it could be dramatically effective. Flavius and Marullus could appeal to it when they rebuke the crowd for so quickly forgetting Pompey (I. 1). It could be an ironic and menacing witness of Caesar's dominance. The producer's final decision may be swayed finally by the practical availability of a good statue.

Brutus and Mark Antony need a raised platform as the pulpit for their speeches. A simple set of rostra can be perfectly effective, and this could also serve as the hill from which Pindarus observes, and misinterprets, the fortunes of Titinius (V. 3).

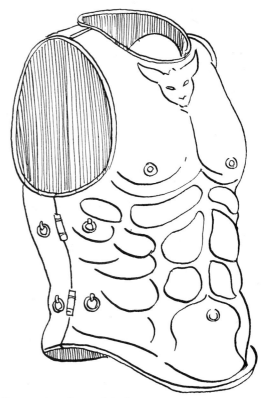

Example of moulded armour

A chair of state for Caesar at the meeting of the Senate (III. 1), and a table with three chairs for the Triumvirs (IV. 1) are the only essential furniture for this part of the play, though chairs or couches and tripods with burning cressets could add atmosphere to the interior of Caesar's house (II. 2).

For the rest of the play, beginning with IV. 2 and continuing to the end, the Roman backcloth could be flown to disclose either a second backcloth, depicting rugged hilly scenery, or a cyclorama on which the lighting could indicate times of day and combine with atmospheric effects. A production at the Northcott Theatre, Exeter, gave a very striking visual expression to the verbal images of Caesar's spirit dominating the action after his death by showing him in the battle scenes by flashes of stroboscopic lighting. This also added effectively to the confusion of battle. The producer might decide that stroboscopic lighting clashed too violently with the Renaissance style of production, but he might still find inspir-

ation in this imaginative and effective use of lighting.

In the latter part of the play, only IV. 3 needs stage furniture. Brutus's tent may be indicated by canvas-type material, draped to suggest three sides and part of the roof. This may be set by soldiers, during IV. 2 and struck by them as the lights come up between Acts IV and V. This can combine easily with the movements of soldiers, indicating the march of the Republican army from Sardis to Philippi. As the last of them leave on one side of the stage, the enemy can enter from the opposite side. The interior of the tent will need a table and four chairs for Brutus and Cassius, Titinius and Messala.

The rostra can remain on stage throughout.

Costume

Caesar's costume should be rich, rather showy and emblematic of power. In I. 2, he should wear a purple cloak over a lorica (cuirass) skirt with labels and buskins. He should also wear an ornamented Roman sword. The sword and breastplate are effective images of his military triumph just as the purple cloak indicates his imperial power. He should also wear a laurel wreath.

For the night scene in his house (II. 2) he would wear an all-enveloping long white night-gown. This is necessary for this scene and will cover the tunic he must wear under his cloak for the assassination, thus making the change easier. He could wear sandals for both scenes.

If the producer decides to show Caesar domi-nating the battle scenes, as in the production mentioned above, it would be suitable for him to return to the more military garb of his first entrance. His Ghost should appear as the living Caesar did in the assassination scene.

Brutus's costume should aim at presenting a slightly self-conscious simplicity, in contrast with Caesar's ostentation. Though this contrast is dramatically essential, it is important that there should be no attempt to use costume to distinguish the conspirators *as a group* until the outbreak of civil war (IV. 1). Any such attempt would flatly contradict the text with its repeated emphasis on deception: 'Let's bear it as our Roman Actors do',

'Hide it in smiles and affability', 'We like friends will go together'. Brutus should, I think, be distinctively civilian until war starts; a cloak draped and fastened at the shoulders so as to suggest a toga, over a tunic with labels on its skirts, and sandals for the first three acts. For the last two, he should wear a lorica with sword belt and sword, buskins and a Roman helmet.

The other Romans should wear the same basic combination of cloak-cum-toga over tunic and sandals for civilian scenes, and helmet, lorica and buskins for war scenes. Differences in rank can be indicated by different insignia and varying degrees of richness. Variations in colour can add greatly to the pictorial effectiveness of the production, and may also be used at times to indicate qualities of temperament. For example, a greenish-yellow tint may suggest the envious nature of Cassius, while opulent and colourful clothing would help to project the sensuous extraversion of Mark Antony. For his first appearance, 'for the course', he would wear only a loincloth or a leopardskin, and carry the traditional thongs of wolfskin with the hair still on.

The tribunes Flavius and Marullus should be dressed identically to indicate the equality of their offices. Their costume should be the same essentially as that of the other nobles with a staff or wand of office. Lucius could wear a plain tunic and sandals.

In IV. 1, the Triumvirs could wear civilian clothes, but it would be quite suitable for them to wear armour in view of the military preparations and the dangers mentioned towards the end of the scene. Their plumed helmets could either lie on the table or, if the producer had several crowd actors, they could be held by attendants in the background. In any case, there should be a sig-nificant contrast among them: Antony as usual should be the most ostentatious; the self-contained, calculating Octavius should be much more plainly though richly dressed; the appearance of Lepidus should suggest, subtly but perceptibly, his lack of real power. His clothes might be slightly ill-fitting, or mix showiness with shabbiness, or mix Antony's style with Octavius's as though he had tried to imitate both.

So far as the crowd is concerned, the sixteenth

The Conspirators

Portia and Calphurnia

Crowd

century London element can be strong here, as in the first scene, at least, this is how Shakespeare seems to have pictured them, and nothing in the later scenes clashes with this. Jerkins and hose, cloaks, tunics, all of rough material for the men. The women would wear the same sort of material made into dresses and cloaks. For both men and women, some would wear sandals, some would be barefoot; some would wear hats.

In the war scenes, the rank and file of the armies, like their civilian equivalents, could be costumed in a markedly Elizabethan style, thus following the example of the Longleat print. In this case, they would wear morions, breastplates, doublets and hose and carry pikes or halberds. Equally well they might be more classically garbed, wearing leather loricas instead of the metal of their superiors.

Two minor but important characters demand special attention: the Soothsayer and Artemidorus. The Soothsayer could wear ordinary Roman civilian plain tunic and cloak. It would, however, be possible to dress him in oriental robes, like a Renaissance painter's idea of one of the three Magi, and would help to suggest the infiltration of Rome by foreign superstition.

For Artemidorus, we could take a hint from Plutarch's description of him as a Greek doctor of rhetoric, that is a Sophist, another foreign influence. The conventional costume of a Greek Sophist would mark him as a foreigner while being historically accurate and within the style of this production.

The two women in the play, Calphurnia and Portia, both appear first in night scenes. For both, therefore, a long nightgown over a long tunic is appropriate, but the wife of Caesar would clearly wear much richer and more elaborate garments than the wife of Brutus and daughter of Cato. This contrast can powerfully reinforce the opposition, of life-style as well as of political principle, between Caesar and Brutus.

In Act II, scene 4, we see Portia with Lucius in the street. Renaissance painters tended to make their women's dresses more contemporary than the men's. A dress that harmonizes with our chosen production style without clashing too violently with the average audience's picture of

ancient Rome would be of soft material, fitting fairly close at the bust and then flowing loosely to the ankles. The sleeves would be loose from shoulder to elbow and tight from elbow to wrist. There might be embroidered bindings to tighten the dress round the neck, under the breasts, and half-way between shoulder and elbow. Over this, she would wear a loose red cloak with a hood.

Props

Many have already been mentioned, others are obvious from the text, but the following are worth mentioning:

II.1 Kerchief — a cloth round the head, an Elizabethan invalid's custom — for Ligarius.

III.1 Swords and daggers for the conspirators, hidden under their cloaks. The text is contradictory about the weapons used. Mark Antony says: 'Look! in this place ran Cassius' dagger through.' (III.2) Yet Cassius says, as he stabs himself (V. 3): 'Caesar, thou art reveng'd. Even with the sword that kill'd thee.'

Like many other contradictions in Shakespeare, this causes no trouble in performance, as the two statements are so far apart that the audience is most unlikely to notice the discrepancy. The producer therefore is free to choose. One practical point is that daggers are obviously easier to hide under robes than are swords.

Lighting

For most of the daylight scenes in the first three acts, the lighting can be simple and straightforward. The first of the night scenes (I.3) demands lightning effects against a dark background. As always, it is essential that effects are strictly subordinate to the words and actions on the stage. For this reason, it is probably wise to concentrate the thunder and lightning effects at the beginning and possibly the end of the scene, with some carefully timed peals and flashes between. Apart from the storm effects, light should be concentrated on one area downstage, to give the effect of a patchily lighted street.

The scene in Brutus's orchard (II. 1) needs

80

Leaders and Philippi

special discretion in this matter. It does occur on the same stormy and portentous night and Brutus speaks of 'The exhalations whizzing in the air', but the tone of the scene is quiet; the conflict at the beginning is internal. All the subject matter calls for a quiet delivery. Only in the last section, from the entrance of Ligarius on, does one feel a need for louder emphasis, and then chiefly in quite short speeches by Ligarius. It fits this interpretation that there is a stage direction for thunder immediately after Ligarius's last speech, only half a line from the end of the scene. For the rest of the scene, Shakespeare underlined the need for quiet by telling us that Lucius is asleep right at the beginning, and again just after the conspirators have left. If, therefore, loud thunder is used at the end of the previous scene, it must die away before Brutus enters. Some flashing effects — for meteors, not lightning — are needed in the early part of the scene. After that, there should be little or nothing until the thunder at the end which leads naturally into the next scene.

The thunder and lightning that end II. 1 should swell to create a powerful beginning to II. 2, but once the effect of shattering storm has been made, the producer must control the machinery carefully and fade out the storm sounds before the end. Where precisely, is a matter for his judgement; he might even decide that a faint but ominous rumble might be atmospherically useful at the end, as the conspirators and Caesar go out together.

At the end of III. 2, flame effects could be used to indicate that the mob have started to carry out their intention of burning Caesar's body 'in the holy place' and setting fire to the conspirators' houses. This would also lead well into the scene of riotous violence that follows. Here the effects of fire and destruction should be intensified. It is easier to avoid the sounds interfering with the words here as, except for Cinna the Poet's brief opening soliloquy, much of the dialogue can quite naturally be spoken loudly or even shouted.

In IV. 2, the opening should suggest at least the approach of evening and be dimmer by the end. The following scene, being inside Brutus's tent,

should have the light concentrated on the acting area downstage, within the limits indicated by the tent structure. As the interior and the onset of night dictate further dimming, it is important to start the previous scene light enough to allow this dimming to be perceptible without hindering a clear view of the actors' faces. The Folio stage direction tells Lucius to bring tapers when he brings the wine. This of course allows the lights to come up until just before the entrance of Caesar's ghost over a hundred lines later, where they must dim ('How ill this taper burns'). The lights should come up again after Caesar's exit.

A possible lighting effect to show Caesar's influence on the battles has already been suggested (page 75).

The last scene is clearly set in dusk or dark. This is confirmed by the reference to torchlight at the beginning of V. 2, and by Brutus's 'Night hands upon mine eyes', a powerfully evocative line.

Sound effects

In addition to the storm (I. 3, II. 1, II. 2) and the lute playing (IV. 3), we have trumpet calls, drum beats and crowd noises. Whereas a sixteenth or seventeenth century production could assume a widespread understanding of ceremonial and military music, and so use it as a system of signals to the audience, a modern producer must, so to speak, create and teach his own system of musical symbols. They must therefore be few and simple. One distinctive trumpet call should be associated with Caesar and used on his ceremonial entrances and exits. In the battle scenes, again there should be distinctive trumpet calls for each of the opposed armies. These can be supported by drum beats to suggest marching armies out of sight but near. Movement can be conveyed very effectively by changing the volume of sound. During the actual fighting, varied and much less measured drum and trumpet sounds can express the turmoil and confusion. Shouted orders, cries and the clash of swords and armour are all essential here.

A production in approximately the historical costume of its own period

Macbeth

⎯⎯⬧⎯⎯

Though a sixteenth century illustration in Holinshed shows Macbeth and Banquo dressed as noblemen of King James I's reign, [1] and Garrick, following the normal conventions of his own era, played Macbeth in eighteenth century dress, and though I have seen a performance in which all the performers were in track suits, [2] *Macbeth* seems a particularly suitable play to present in the setting and costume of its own period – the middle of the eleventh century. We may, however, allow ourselves the licence of using the theatrically effective winged or horned helmets, which historically belong to a slightly earlier period, and rather to the Norwegian invaders than to the Scottish defenders.

A word of warning about these winged helmets may prove useful. It is essential that all entrances are high enough and wide enough to allow all helmet-wearers to pass in and out freely, and that they have plenty of practice so that they move both confidently and without unseemly collisions. I stress this because I have vivid memories of a first night of *Macbeth* where these precautions had obviously been neglected, with the result that hardly an entrance or an exit took place without a wing of the very splended helmets catching on the doorway and twisting or tilting the helmet to a rakish but dramatically inappropriate angle. The most unfortunate misadventure to a helmet came near the climax of the tragedy, Macbeth's hand to hand fight with Macduff. The producer had clearly decided to add originality to the stereotyped clashing of sword on sword and sword on shield. After a fairly conventional opening, therefore, Macduff struck Macbeth's sword out of his hand. Macbeth retaliated by hurling his shield at his enemy – to be precise, dropping it rather limply at his feet. Then came what we all realized was to be the great moment of the fight. Macbeth seized the horns of his helmet – naturally the most magnificent of all – obviously intending to hurl that too at Macduff in a last grand gesture of defiance. Unfortunately the helmet did not budge. With increasing desperation, he tried twisting it from right to left, and from left to right. He tried pulling down with one hand while pushing up with the other, first this side, then that. All this time the unfortunate actor playing Macduff was dancing round him, trying to look as though there was some reason why he should not close in for the kill at once. At last, with a final two-handed heave, Macbeth wrenched the helmet from his head – and his wig came with it.

Up to this point, we in the audience had restrained ourselves with sympathetic self-control, but then the floodgates burst, and surely the black tragedy of *Macbeth* has never ended to such gales of laughter. This was indeed an object lesson in the necessity of adequate rehearsal, especially when unusual costume and special stage business are concerned.

These misadventures might also, of course, be regarded as evidence of the traditional unluckiness of *Macbeth*. Perhaps this legend arose from the direct invocations to the powers of evil in the play and from their prominent part in it. Certainly it was strongly believed by old actors I knew, some of whom would not even name it directly but referred to it as 'Shakespeare's Scotch play' Fortunately there have been plenty of trouble-free productions of *Macbeth*, and I hope the legend will not deter any company from producing it. The atmosphere of evil, however, is essential, and I must now justify my choice of an approximately eleventh century setting as particularly suitable to assist the performance in conveying this atmosphere to the audience.

While a sixteenth or seventeenth century setting may well be defended on the grounds that this was the great era of witch hunts and witch trials all over Western Europe and the North American colonies, there are other aspects of the play that point to an earlier, more primitive age. Macbeth's almost superhuman prowess as a warrior show him in the heroic age. He triumphs in battle not by superior tactics or by leading a better equipped and disciplined army, but because, as the Bleeding Sergeant reports, he

> Disdaining Fortune, with his brandish'd steel,
> Which smoked with bloody execution,
> Like Valour's minion carv'd out his passage,
> Till he faced the slave;
> Which ne'er shook hands, nor bade farewell
> to him,
> Till he unseamed him from the nave to
> th' chaps
> And fixed his head upon our battlements.
> (I. 2 17-23)

Later in the same scene, Ross, another eyewitness of his prowess, re-emphasizes his heroic stature by calling him 'Bellona's bridegroom', thus comparing Macbeth directly with Mars, the war god himself. And this greatness as a warrior remains with him to the end, after all his other virtues have been corrupted. We are meant, I think, to accept the Apparition's prophecy that he is indeed invincible except by the one man chosen by destiny to conquer and kill him.

The Weird Sisters are ambiguous creatures. We may reject the Romantic extravagances that described them as Fates or Norns. However great their influence, Shakespeare makes it clear that Macbeth finally makes his own decisions. However, we must admit they have many of the traditional characteristics that Shakespeare's contemporaries associated with witches. Their answers to Paddock and Graymalkin (I. 1. 7-8) imply they had a toad and a cat as their familiars. They kill farm animals and avenge insults by raising storms (I. 3. 1-25). Unlike ordinary witches, however, they seem to have no ordinary local habitation. They describe themselves as 'Posters of the sea and land' as though their territory was boundless. It is true that Macbeth knows where to find them (III. 4. 132-3) and (IV. 1), but even this cavern, apart from its dramatic value, seems a place for compounding potions and raising spirits rather than a dwelling. Banquo, the first human to see them, emphasizes the contradictory elements in their appearance:

> What are these,
> So withered, and so wild in their attire
> That look not like th' inhabitants o' the'
> earth,
> And yet are on 't...
> You should be women,
> And yet your beards forbid to interpret
> That you are so. (I. 3. 39-47)

These are some of the element of *Macbeth* that lead one to set it in a past where history and legend, heroic warriors and grotesque incarnations of evil are congruent with magnificent poetry and realistic touches of everyday life.

There are over thirty speaking parts in *Macbeth*, though a medium-sized company can manage with well-organized doubling and trebling.

So far as the title role is concerned, *Macbeth* makes the hardest of all Shakespeare's demands on his leading man. This was the opinion of Robert Atkins, most experienced of Shakespearian producers, and it is supported by the fact that no Shakespearian actor has ever been primarily famed for his Macbeth, as many have been for their Hamlets, several for their Othellos and a few for the apparently more formidable challenge of Lear. The essential difficulty lies in reconciling the epic physical strength and courage of the hero who

The Weird Sisters

'carved out his passage' with a sword 'which smoked with bloody execution' with the paralysing vividness of his imagination. 'Present fears Are less than horrible imaginings' (I. 3. 137-8) gives the essence of his character. There is also the technical problem mentioned by one of the most striking modern Macbeths, Sir Laurence Olivier: the sheer difficulty of keeping enough breath and vocal power for the last great speeches.

Actor and producer would probably be best advised not to agonize over reconciling the warrior and the poet in Macbeth, but simply to play each scene and speak each speech as well as possible, leaving the total effect to Shakespeare.

The other parts are comparatively easy for any competent Shakespearian performer. Lady Macbeth, for example, has come in all sizes from the majestic Sarah Siddons to the petite Helen Faucit. Power she certainly must have, but the basic picture is simple: a will that is strong enough to drive her husband to murder but also to drive herself to breakdown and probably to suicide.

Ross has more subtlety than he is usually given in performance. He is essentially a courtier, whose judgement is shrewd enough to square his conscience with the powers that be — or are going to be. He seems to accept Macbeth's kingship until the tyranny goes too far and the tide turns against it. Then he joins Malcolm. Yet there is no suggestion of hypocrisy.

Banquo presents a similar moral dilemma in a stronger form and one harder to project theatrically today. There is no doubt we are meant to take him as a virtuous character. This is clear both from the internal evidence and from the fact that legend made him the ancestor of King James VI of Scotland, who was an early spectator of *Macbeth*. Obviously, Shakespeare would not present his royal patron's ancestor in an unflattering light.

Yet there is one scene where Banquo's behaviour is ambiguous to our eyes. His opening soliloquy in Act I, scene 3 says:

Thou hast it now — King, Cawdor, Glamis, all
As the weird women promis'd; and I fear
Thou play'dst most foully for it.

He goes on to hope that the promises of royalty held out to his descendants may prove equally true. When Macbeth appears, Banquo treats him with the respect due to a lawful sovereign. Many modern spectators have felt here that Banquo must be a time-server, ready to accept a murderous usurper to ensure the succession of his own posterity — hardly the noble character he appears elsewhere. A contemporary audience might have found no problem here. According to one widely accepted theory, the ceremony of coronation, with all its religious implications, gave legitimacy even to a usurper. With one vital exception, all his countrymen owed him full allegiance. The exception, of course, was the legitimate heir to the throne. Once Malcolm took the field to claim his inheritance, he was justified, and so were all who supported him. Until then, obedience was due to the anointed king — Macbeth. The theory is clear enough, but impossible for the subtlest actor to convey to an audience who know nothing about it. Only a programme note can help here.

Malcolm himself can be a far more impressive character on stage than in text. Marius Goring's performance in this part, as long ago as 1934, is still vivid in my mind. By sheer dignity of bearing and clear verse-speaking, he came near to stealing the show from such formidable competitors as Charles Laughton and Flora Robson.

Settings

The suggestions that follow are suitable for any type of stage of reasonable size and equipment but the equipment must include at least one trap with apparatus for raising and lowering the cauldron.

The action of *Macbeth* takes place in three basic settings: castle, interior and exterior; a cave; an open heath, and a number of unspecified exteriors.

With minor changes of decorative emblems and furniture, the same set can serve for all castle scenes. The bare essentials of the castle set are battlements, a large central entrance, and a staircase. These can be provided by a series of flats upstage and parallel to the back wall, with a central archway and practical double gates, and a flight of 'stone' steps leading from left or right of the arch up into the wings on that side. The walls, painted to look like stone slabs, and with battlemented tops, can represent either the outer or the inner walls of whatever castle is required for a particular scene. A curtain may be lowered to hide the battlements for interior scenes. The staircase can serve Macbeth for his fatal ascent to Duncan's room and Lady Macbeth's sleep-walking scene. The sides can continue the style of the back wall to form a box-set; they can use ordinary or revolving flats, or they can simply be draped with black hangings. In any case, there will be at least two entrances on each side at ground level as well as the central gate and the entrance from above via the steps. The producer may introduce many variations into this basic pattern. There may be different degrees of elaboration in the wall and gate, as long as the essential massiveness is not lost: a rounded Norman arch with rough dog-tooth ornament, double doors giving the impression of heavy wood, bound with iron, and with heavy iron bars and lock. There could be a platform level with the bottom of the battlements, to provide a suitable look-out position for any sentinels the producer might want to use; and it could add to the general effect of wide and violent action in the final battle scenes. The possibly rather dull straight line of the castle wall at the back might be broken by setting the doorway either up or down of the main line. Instead being straight, the steps might have a landing dividing them into two parts at an angle to each other. Other variations might come to the producer's own mind or be suggested to him, or perhaps even forced on him, by the particular conditions of his stage. Many highly successful ideas have resulted from having to solve awkward problems posed by unavoidable material conditions.

The open heath where we first meet the Weird Sisters and the various open spaces where we see the Scottish nobles gathering for their attack on Macbeth can all be represented by the fore-part of the stage: the lighting can concentrate on this so that the castle is unnoticed. Alternatively, the castle may be flown. If within the resources of the theatre, these scenes may be played before a drop curtain suitably painted to represent desolate open country. Groundrows are a further elaboration that the producer might like to use.

The cavern where the Weird Sisters call up the Apparitions to answer Macbeth's questions demands more technical care. It needs a trap for the cauldron to sink into — 'Why sinks that cauldron?' Macbeth asks — and for the Apparitions to rise from. It must also at least suggest the enclosed feeling of a cavern. Skilfully concentrated lighting can, in fact, produce this effect very well, especially as the flames under the cauldron and the special lighting of the Apparitions focus the audience's attention on the centre of the action, so that the contrast with the surrounding darkness is enough to convey the impression of being closed in and cut off from the outside world. If a more concrete kind of scenery is desired, of course, an inset of painted canvas to represent the interior of a cave may be used. The text indicates the gruesome ingredients of the hellbroth in sufficient detail.

We now come to consider the castle scenes in detail and to suggest how they may be differentiated sufficiently to show the audience all they need to follow the action easily without encumbering the swift movement of this play with unnecessary setting and striking of furniture and props.

Act I, scene 4 is the first of four scenes in the palace of Forres. It is an official scene, where King Duncan is dealing with the aftermath of defeated rebellion and invasion. Though short, this is a turning point in the play; partly because it reveals Duncan making precisely the same error in trusting Macbeth, the new Thane of Cawdor, that he had made in trusting his freshly executed predecessor; even more because by recognizing Malcolm as his heir, he inadvertently dashes Macbeth's only hope of becoming king legitimately. The King could sit on one of a pair of thrones set on a dais fairly well down-stage. The thrones should be the kind we see in eleventh and twelfth century pictures: gold-painted wood ornamented with small orbs. They should have arms, more or less ornate according to the wishes of the producer. The backs should be carved, perhaps with a dogtooth pattern, perhaps with a heraldic Scottish lion. The seats should have red velvet cushions, preferably with gold fringes. The second throne has the practical convenience that the same pair will serve for the scenes showing Macbeth and his wife in their state, and it also has the dramatic value of increasing sympathy for Duncan by emphasizing his loneliness. For a speedy change, the thrones could be fixed to a dais with lockable wheels.

Banners with the royal arms of Scotland may be set in iron holders on each of the central gates, or they may be held there by guards. This may prove enough, with a well grouped body of nobles and soldiers, to give sufficient weight and ceremony to the scene. An optional extra would be a small writing table and stool for a clerk to record the King's decisions. If this is desired, both should be of plain wood and of very simple construction, and set with parchment, quill pen and silver inkhorn.

For the remaining scenes at Forres the following changes are needed. For III. 1, the only difference is the need to open the gates for the processional entrance of Macbeth 'as King' and Lady Macbeth 'as Queen'. These stage directions, supported by the 'Sennet sounded', clearly emphasize the ceremonial nature of this, their first royal appearance. The producer will probably want to make use of the greatest possible number of his company, enhancing the effect by making full use of the different stage levels.

For scene 2, the set remains the same, but both the imagery and Macbeth's specific statement:

> Light thickens, and the crow
> Makes wing to th' rooky wood:
> Good things of day begin to droop and
> drowse,
> Whiles night's black agents to their preys
> do rouse

indicate darker lighting. This is mainly for stage lighting to create, but torches in iron holders on the walls or cressets on iron tripods will be needed too.

Act III, scene 4 of course needs a totally different atmosphere. It is clearly an official state banquet attended by nearly all the great nobles of Scotland.

The two thrones on their dais will face down along the length of a banqueting table, set with plates, goblets and food. How much and how realistic this table-dressing will be depends on the producer's general concept of the production and on how he visualizes the opening of the scene. It

can begin with the table fully set and the actors on stage, or it can begin, perhaps more effectively, with servants putting the final touches to the table, and then a ceremonial procession through the centre entrance. Convenience of striking the set may be helped by having some of the dishes fixed to the table, so that there is no danger of their falling off during setting and striking. Long benches for most of the guests are in period and much easier to move than chairs, though there must be a stool for Banquo.

This scene presents an interesting challenge to the company's lighting expert. It calls for an effect of barbaric splendour and yet there must not be an atmosphere of genuine festivity. Light may be concentrated on what the audience needs to see, while the surrounding area is in a darkness from which the murderer and Banquo's ghost can make their sinister entrances.

The interior of Macduff's castle (IV. 2) calls for another contrast. Fear and horror are there, but the actors should be able to create them all the more effectively against a background of innocent domesticity. The action should be well downstage, so that the wall is just visible enough to suggest a castle without too clear a reminder of Forres. A low and fairly simple wooden chair for Lady Macduff and a stool for her son are the essential furniture, but a spinning wheel would help the domestic atmosphere.

Quite a different sort of contrast is required for the exterior of Edward the Confessor's castle (IV. 3). Shakespeare presents the court of 'the most pious Edward' as a place of sanctity and light against the diabolical darkness of Macbeth's Scotland. The whole scene should be much lighter. The castle gates should be open, suggesting that here is a place where people do not need to be perpetually on guard. The royal arms of England should be displayed on each side of the gates. No more is necessary, but a bench or two may be placed downstage if the producer or the actors feel uncomfortable at standing for the whole scene.

The remaining castle scenes are all in Dunsinane, where the atmosphere is one of increasing doom. The first, Lady Macbeth's sleep-walking scene (V. 1), demands the minimum of light that will allow the audience to follow what is happening. A

Duncan Banquo and Macbeth

small area of light downstage on the far side from the staircase for the Physician and the Gentlewoman and a spot to follow Lady Macbeth should be enough. No furniture is necessary, but the producer might consider the ironic effect of Lady Macbeth's sitting on the throne during her mental agony.

For scenes 3 and 5, Dunsinane can be set much as Forres in III. 1. All that the audience needs is the picture of a castle as background to the words and action. The gates must obviously be shut. Macbeth certainly needs the throne to give visual support to the great speeches that express the hollowness of his kingship and his life.

The throne must be struck for scene 6. Macbeth's banner should still hang from the battlements and the gates must still be shut.

From scene 7 on to the end, the gates are open, and no other change is needed. The effects here are for the actors, sound and props; the scenic artist has done his work.

Costume

The basic male garments for peacetime were tunic and trousers or hose. The tunics varied from just above knee-length to nearly ankle length, and might be plain or have collars, borders and belts in contrasting colours. The hose often matched these decorative contrasts and sometimes had variegated stripes of their own. Shoes usually did not rise above the ankles. Cloaks, too, varied from just below knee-length to ankle-length; the shorter ones were usually fastened with a large round brooch on the right shoulder, the longer ones with a brooch under the throat. The most common civilian headgear was like a close-fitting beret. Shakespeare seems to have pictured the Scots as wearing blue bonnets or caps (see Falstaff's reference to 'a thousand blue-caps more' in Henry IV, Part One, II. 4. 347-8). Even if this may be an anachronism for the eleventh century, it may still be useful for a producer to observe, and will be one way of supporting Malcolm's line 'My countryman but yet I know him not' (IV. 3. 160) which implies something distinctively Scottish about Ross's dress. Servants wear tunic and hose indoors, plus cloaks outside.

The royal insignia include a crown and sceptre, as well as a richer robe. The essence of the crown in Western Europe was a circlet of gold with ornamental sprigs rising from it: these might be crosses or, as the Bayeux Tapestry shows us, trefoils. The sceptre is a similarly ornamented gold baton. Like the crown, it may be jewelled if the producer wants a richer effect. The orb, a plain gold ball surmounted by a cross, and a Sword of State may also be set on stage or carried by attendants on the three state scenes (I. 4, III. 1 and III. 4). The Sword of State should be longer than a practical fighting sword, with gold and jewelled hilt and ornamental scabbard, perhaps of gold-bound velvet.

The armour of the higher ranks will consist of a chainmail hauberk reaching almost to the knee; sword-belt and sword, shield and winged helmet. There will be plenty of room for variations on this basic pattern. Soldiers of lower rank can wear conical helmets, leather helmets, drabber hose and carry spears.

Macbeth needs four basic costumes: armour for his early and his last appearances; royal robes for III. 1 and III. 4; and what we may call ordinary civilian clothes for the remainder, except for II. 3 when he must wear a nightgown. Changes could be multiplied: he might have two suits of armour, one battered and stained for the early scenes, where he is supposed to be fresh from the battlefield, another new and more magnificent, when he is the King and about to fight. Similarly, he might wear different civilian clothes in different scenes, though here the changes might be merely partial, such as a change of cloak or belt. On the other hand, one could simplify to the utmost by dressing him throughout in the same tunic and gross-gartered trousers, over which he could wear, according to need, his hauberk, sword-belt and helmet, or his crown and royal cloak. On the whole, simplicity works better, is cheaper, and less distracting to the actor than endless changes. Crimson and black seem the colours that express him best.

Malcolm and Donaldbain could be dressed alike, with a prevailing emphasis on green, the colour of youth and returning life. The difference in age, and consequently in status, can be indicated by richer decoration on Malcolm's dress. Fleance and

Lady Macbeth. Front and back view of costume

young Macduff could be similarly though less richly dressed.

In pattern, Banquo's dress should be like Macbeth's, but an emphasis on white and gold would point the moral contrast. The other thanes would also wear much the same clothes as Macbeth and Banquo, only less rich. Macduff, of course, must stand out somewhat. A combination of red and white might suggest his combining innocence with just vengeance, as well as linking him with the Apparition of the Bleeding Child 'from his mother's womb Untimely ripped'. As we are keeping, though with some licence, to the costume of the historic period of Macbeth, there is no need to distinguish sharply between the armour of the Scottish thanes and that of the English leaders, Siward and his son: their shields can show some difference if desired.

The basic pattern of the ladies' wear is clearly illustrated in the two views of Lady Macbeth (page 91): a long gown, high-necked, close-fitting down to the waist, and flowing loosely from a low belt.

Lady Macbeth's first entrance (I. 5) could be in a comparatively simple version, the everyday wear of a great lady. The dress could be plain green, with a gold belt and ornamental neckband. For I. 6 and I. 7 and II. 2, where she is the King's hostess, there could be either a complete change into a more elaborately ornamented robe of blue and gold, with the addition of necklet and bracelet of gold, set with rubies and emeralds, or she could keep the same dress and simply add the ornaments. In II. 3 she must wear a night-gown, as in her sleep-walking scene. Her State appearances (III. 1 and III. 4) could again call for either a complete change into royal robes of crimson and gold, or she could just add a crown and a fur-lined cloak to her previous dress. In the other domestic scenes, she could revert to her first costume.

Lady Macduff would wear the same pattern of dress, little different from Lady Macbeth's first costume. A predominance of violet and white might suggest innocence combined with vulnerability.

The Waiting Gentlewoman would wear a grey nightgown over a white ankle-length shift.

If the producer wished to have more ladies-in-waiting, and had enough performers to provide them, they would wear plainer versions of their mistress's robes.

Macbeth addresses the Weird Sisters as 'secret, black and midnight hags' (IV. 1) and this indicates the essential nature of their costume. Long black cloaks, possibly hooded, over long black or dark grey dresses seem the most suitable for them. They have the added theatrical advantage that they make it easier for the Weird Sisters to appear mysteriously from and fade back into the darkness.

The three Apparitions in IV. 1 are usually represented by images raised and lowered from the cauldron. The First must obviously have a helmet exactly similar to Macbeth's. The 'show of eight kings' may either be presented by a procession of eight robed and crowned actors or they may be created in the audience's imagination by Macbeth's words and reactions, possibly assisted by flickering shadows. Banquo's ghost had better appear in either case. If the procession is invisible to the audience, the smiling though 'blood-boltered Banquo' will give valuable support to Macbeth's words in projecting the image.

Props

Most of the hand-props have been mentioned in the appropriate scenes, but we must add the following: a letter for Lady Macbeth (I. 5), plates of food and flagons for servants to carry across the stage in I. 7); carryable torches for Macbeth's servant in II. 1 and for Fleance in III. 3; leafy boughs for Malcolm's army to carry when they enter at the beginning of V. 6. Finally, a model of Macbeth's head, possibly on a pole. This can be made a good likeness by making a papier mâché mask of Macbeth's face and using it as a mould for a wax image. If the producer considers this unnecessarily gruesome, Macduff can easily point to the battlement, where we may imagine 'Th' usurper's cursed head' to be placed.

Special effects

Special effects, both visual and sound, are particularly numerous and important in *Macbeth*. By far the most important are those connected with the Apparitions rising from the cauldron.

The Apparitions themselves may be masks or models. Masks have the advantage of being easier to make and less liable to damage. Whichever is chosen, the images can be fixed to poles and raised and lowered either mechanically or by someone standing immediately below the trap. Machines have an unfortunate tendency to go wrong at the vital moment, so a human agent is preferable. Careful practice is needed to ensure smooth movement up and down.

There must be lighting below the stage to give the effect of flickering flames (see drawing page 85).

Whether Banquo's ghost is presented as a 'real' ghost or, like the air-borne dagger in II. 1, a figment of Macbeth's imagination, is for the producer to decide. Furthermore, if he chooses to have a 'real' ghost, he still has to decide how like the living Banquo he is to be. Clearly he must be recognizable: there are acceptable variations, though, from merely adding some bloodstains to the face and head of the actor to giving him a much more blood spattered mask with equally gory wig attached. On the whole, the latter fits Macbeth's description better, and therefore seems preferable provided that the likeness is not lost.

Sound effects are mostly musical and are clearly indicated in the text. They are vital to create the varied impressions of court ceremony, magic and battle.

Lighting

This, too, is especially important as it can do so much to convey the pervading colour of *Macbeth*: darkness broken by flickering lights that show the gold of royalty and the red of blood. The producer must therefore ensure the closest co-operation of scenic artist and lighting expert so that the lighting brings out to the full all the effects that the scenery has been designed to convey.

A permanent set with late Elizabethan dress

Hamlet

Hamlet is a tragedy that has become part of the world's mythology, and yet it is so deeply embedded in its own period that no other can supply an equally appropriate setting.

From its earliest appearance, *Hamlet* has been one of the main pillars of Shakespeare's fame. Three Quartos were printed in his lifetime and two more shortly after. Harold Child remarks in the New Cambridge edition that its stage history would fill several books. Nearly every great actor in this country, from Burbage to Jonathan Pryce, has played Hamlet. Few months pass without a book or learned article on some aspect of the hero or the play. Perhaps never a day passes without people otherwise ignorant of Shakespeare saying 'To be or not be be'. There is a genuine though comic tribute to its fame in the story of the naive spectator who commented, after seeing a performance, that he didn't think much of *Hamlet* as it was all made up of old quotations. Nor is its fame confined to England or English-speaking countries: a German version may have been performed as early as 1616; outstandingly valuable studies have come from Germany, Spain and Poland. Critical interpretations have been equally numerous: Hamlet has been considered a portrait of the Earl of Essex, with Polonius as a satire on William Cecil, Lord Burghley; as a type of the Melancholy Man; of the man of thought overwhelmed by the world of action; as a self-portrait

of the author. He has been interestingly, though not convincingly, psychoanalyzed by the doyen of English Freudians, Dr Ernest Jones. In spite of all this, there is perhaps no Shakespearian play more deeply rooted in its own time. Hamlet's political position is clear only if we know what the early seventeenth century thought was the proper way of inheriting a kingdom. We cannot fully understand his personal problems unless we have some knowledge of the then current beliefs about the next world and the nature of ghosts, and of the clash between the ethic of revenge and the Christian ethic of forgiveness. The obligations of filial piety are equally important to understanding Hamlet's duty to his father and Ophelia's to Polonius. Much of Hamlet's talk with the players, especially the reference to the Wars of the Theatres, needs some knowledge of theatrical history. Even so dramatically vital a scene as the duel can be hard for a modern audience to follow without special knowledge.

At this point, the reader may well ask how the play can have been so long and so widely popular if it calls for so much special knowledge. Surely there is a contradiction somewhere? The most important answer is that, in spite of the vast changes in political systems, in ethics and in social customs that separate us from the seventeenth century, there remains an even vaster amount of common ground. Shakespeare dug so deeply that he found this common ground over and over again. Though, for example, the precise moral codes of his England may seem historical curiosities, we are still familiar with the ideas of forgiveness and revenge and with the conflicting urges to both. Parental authority may be a shadow of itself, but the ideal of filial obligation is still felt, if only to be rejected. Political power no longer normally centres in royal courts, even where they exist, but the power itself is greater than ever, and the means of gaining it, holding it and exercising it have changed more in appearance than in reality. Emotionally, there is nothing remote in Hamlet's essential situation as a young man deprived of his proper place and betrayed — or at least, believing himself to be betrayed — by the two women he had loved and trusted: 'There needs no ghost, my lord, come from the grave/To tell us this.'

The Ghost itself is harder for a modern audience to take seriously in quite the same way, but a reasonably sympathetic spectator would find it as easy to accept as a convention from the past as he would the ruffs and doublets of a seventeenth century style production. This really is the second answer: to accept certain differences of convention in belief and behaviour is not necessarily harder than to accept the convention of blank verse. A spectator who will not or cannot make such adjustments should stay away. Even more emphatically, a company unwilling to make them should not touch Shakespeare.

Finally, one must admit that there are a few passages whose *full* meaning will be lost without explanation. The references to the Wars of the Theatres are a good example. Even here, the essential point dramatically is the fickleness of public taste; and this is clear even to an audience that does not know that the 'little eyasses' were the temporarily successful companies of boy actors. Moreover, the exceptional length of *Hamlet* usually calls for some cuts. This is always a pity, but if cuts must be made, they might as well exclude passages that are both dramatically inessential and difficult for the average audience to follow.

In many material details, the play specifically refers to contemporary customs, costumes and weapons. At the Ghost's first appearance, Marcellus asks: 'Shall I strike at it with my partisan?' Admittedly, the partisan is still carried by the Yeoman of the Guard at the Tower of London, but the sentinels on duty at Elsinore are clearly meant to be effective soldiers, not picturesque survivals. There is repeated insistence that the Ghost is 'clad in complete steel', wearing 'his beaver (visor) up', and this is not a mere striking visual effect: it conveyed that the Ghost comes to warn or inform of evil. Barnardo suggests a connection with the threatened war, and later Hamlet explicitly says, 'my father's spirit *in arms* (my italics), all is not well'. The duel, which brings Hamlet his triumph as well as his death, is much easier to perform under Elizabethan than modern rules of fencing. However trustful Hamlet might be, it would be hard for him not to notice the absence of the protective button from a modern foil; the difference between a sharp and a blunt rapier would be much less obvious. The essential business of exchanging swords, though it has been done successfully with modern foils, is much easier with rapier and dagger. The duelling dagger was often provided with hooks near the hilt for the express purpose of gripping the opponent's blade and twisting it out of his grip.

Altogether then, despite the interesting possibilities of other period styles, and the success they have achieved, *Hamlet* seems particularly suited to an Elizabethan production.

Setting

The setting must be flexible enough to serve as the battlements and other undefined outer parts of the castle, and a variety of public and private rooms and corridors within. The plan that follows combines these needs with simplicity of design and construction.

Upstage, a platform with turrets at each end. Above the platform, a backcloth or cyclorama on which lighting can produce any desired sky effect. Below the platform, a painted stone wall with double gates to give a large central entrance. Leading from stage left of the platform a broad flight of shallow stairs down to the level of the main stage, On the right, and fairly well down stage, a dais with two or three steps, with two thrones set on it. A trapdoor is needed down-stage, both for the Ghost's disappearance into the 'cellarage' and for Ophelia's grave. These are the bare essentials.

Apart from the two thrones, which might well remain set throughout to emphasize the play's political dimension, other furniture could easily be set and struck, either openly in view of the audience, or under cover of darkness or behind curtains. The only scene that might present any difficulty is the Queen's Closet scene (III. 4) where, in addition to the bed or couch and chairs, there must be the arras for Polonius to hide behind. This must be a strong enough to stand the strain of Hamlet's stabbing through it and of Polonius's falling through it. It could be hung from a rail secured to solid parts of the scenery: in the angle formed by the back wall and the side of the steps.

At somewhat greater cost, both in money and mechanical devices, one could have a heavy velvet-type curtain in red, either flown or drawn, to hide the back wall for the indoor scenes.

Costume

Nearly all of us have a general picture of English costume at the turn of the sixteenth to the seventeenth century. For younger more fashionable men, a plumed velvet cap, cloak and doublet with ruff, trunk hose from waist to thigh, tighter hose below, and decoratively slashed shoes. For older men, similar but less fancifully decorated garments, and much longer cloaks. For ladies, a tight-fitting bodice, also with ruff, and, most distinctive of all, the farthingale.

On this fundamental pattern, there can be endless variations of colours, shape, detail and decoration, to express differences of rank and character. Colour is partly a matter of the total visual effect, to be worked out by producer, dress designer and scenic artist in close cooperation; it is also an important way of expressing the wearer's character. In shape and detail, the cloak may be collared or collarless, longer or shorter, draped evenly or over one shoulder, and its lining may contrast with the outer colour. Hats could be rakishly tilted and elegantly feathered; look like forerunners of the top-hat; or could be uncompromisingly round and plain.

The doublet may or may not have a basque. By the time of *Hamlet*, it could be boned into the somewhat grotesque peascod shape. It could have its own sleeves or it could end at the shoulders in picadils to display contrasting shirt sleeves. Ruffs could vary greatly, in size, number of layers, and in detailed decoration. Similarly, the trunk hose might vary in fullness and in length, in prominence of codpiece, and in decoration, particularly in the colour and pattern of the panes. The canions or upper stockings were often decoratively embroidered, while the netherstocks, from the knee down, were comparatively plain. Chains, jewels and gloves were accessories of social and therefore of dramatic importance.

With the obvious exception of colour and jewellery, the chief variations in ladies' dress were the style of ruff, the degree of décolleté, the style of sleeve, and the decorative possibilities of opening the skirt in front to show a contrasting underskirt.

Given the basic patterns of Elizabethan costume, most of the details follow logically. There are, however, a few points that should be mentioned. The contrast between Hamlet's 'nighted colour' and 'inky cloak' on the one hand and the luxury and magnificence of the Danish court on the other is of vital dramatic importance. It is one of the most striking examples of Shakespeare's supporting words and actions with powerful visual effects. He tells us this clearly at Hamlet's first appearance, and we must never forget it or allow the audience to do so.

Two variations on Hamlet's first appearance in his 'inky cloak' and 'customary suits of solemn black' are essential. In some scenes, his dress must be disordered enough to justify Ophelia's description of him and the general impression of his madness. The amount of disorder must depend on exactly how Hamlet's state of mind is conceived. Is he wholly sane, though at times pretending to be mad? Or is he just sane, but near to and occasionally over the border of sanity? Or are there times when he really suffers the madness that he claims to be assuming? All are possible and practicable interpretations, and each could express itself in differing degrees of disorder in Hamlet's dress.

A second, quite different variation is in the

Hamlet, King, Queen, Polonius and Ophelia

graveyard scene (V. 1) where a rough seaman's cloak suits his sudden return by sea and explains why he is not immediately recognized. It also gives added dramatic force to the moment when he announces himself. As he steps from the shadows, he can throw off the cloak as he proclaims 'This is I – Hamlet the Dane.' It is worth noting here that in this context 'the Dane' was no mere, and superfluous, statement of nationality: it meant 'the King of Denmark'. To say it to Claudius's face was to brand him a usurper and to claim Denmark as Hamlet's lawful realm: an emphatic sign that the Hamlet who had returned was in some vital matters a changed man – harder, more determined, altogether more formidable.

Claudius would wear a long, obviously royal robe, at least in the official scenes, such as I. 2 and II. 2 (to receive his ambassadors) and probably to watch 'The Murder of Gonzago' and the duel. He would also wear the sash and medallion of some order, traditionally the Danish Order of the Elephant, around his neck. Scene two of Act one is the most official and ceremonial scene of the whole play; here at least, he must wear his crown. At all times his apparel should be 'rich not gaudy'; proclaiming, not the man, but the image he is shrewd enough to project. If it is part of the director's vision of the play to see Claudius more through Hamlet's eyes than is customary, he could use costume to imply the contrast between image and reality. He could be slightly overdressed, he could be given gestures, even perhaps a looking glass, to indicate self-consciousness. His clothes, though magnificent, might be slightly too big for him, thus using the imagery describing another usurper, Macbeth, whose title hangs 'loose about him, like a giant's robe/Upon a dwarfish thief.' Such a strategy would need great tact in the execution. Claudius must never be made insignificant, still less ridiculous. Shakespeare shows him a skilful and successful diplomatist in his dealings with Norway; courageous and quick witted in turning Laertes's murderous rage against him into a cunning and nearly successful means of destroying Hamlet; attractive enough sexually to win Gertrude's love from her husband and, so far as the evidence goes, genuinely devoted to her. Apart from the director's own interpretation, much will depend upon the physique of the actor playing Claudius. It is always better to work with nature than against it.

Laertes, Rosencrantz and Guildenstern are all fashionably dressed young men, but differences in dress can indicate both psychological and social contrasts that are also dramatically effective. In his father's presence, Laertes would hardly ignore his recommendation of a sober rather than a flamboyant richness. For the farewell scene (I. 3), he might change completely into plainer clothes, or his situation as a traveller might be shown simply by wearing or carrying a travelling cloak and changing his court shoes for knee boots. On his violent entrance into the palace (IV. 5), a drawn sword and some dishevelment are obviously needed. A black cloak and hat would suffice for his mourning at Ophelia's funeral. For the duel, he could return to the more formal court costume of his first appearance.

Rosencrantz and Guildenstern could be very similarly dressed, as a sort of rather sinister Tweedledum and Tweedledee. In this case, they should, I think, be slightly, but only slightly, overdressed; to suggest they were trying just a little too hard and, more subtly, to hint at the inner emptiness that made them easy, if perhaps innocent, tools of Claudius. On the other hand, director and actors might want to make the most of the small but noticeable distinctions that appear between them. Both in their attempted interrogation of Hamlet (II. 2) and in their report of it to the King, Guilderstern seems slightly the more honest or perhaps merely the clumsier liar: Rosencrantz lies more fluently and, significantly, receives the more bitter contempt from Hamlet in IV. 2. If these differences are to be stressed, costume can play its part. Rosencrantz should be perceptibly the sleeker and slicker in dress as well as in behaviour.

By far the most overdressed of all, of course, is Osric. His clothes should be colourful to the point of gaudiness, while 'water-fly' suggest lightness as well as brightness. Dover Wilson's suggestion of a winged doublet and the most elaborately plumed and decorated hat is valuable.

When analyzed, the character of Horatio presents certain puzzles. In the first scene, Marcellus and Barnardo appeal to him successfully for inside information about Denmark's military preparations. He speaks of Hamlet's father as *'our* (my italics) last king'. Yet, in I. 4, Hamlet has to explain the drinking habits of the Danish court as to a stranger, and he says he saw Hamlet senior 'once'. Again, he is obviously Hamlet's closest friend, the one person Hamlet can trust, yet he has been at the court for at least some weeks without any meeting. Like so many Shakespearian puzzles, these appear only when one studies the play and are hardly ever noticed in performance. Nevertheless, there are some problems about Horatio that directly affect his costume. He is clearly not rich and he has suffered misfortune. Hamlet refers to both of these in III. 2. We know also that he is a scholar. Some producers have interpreted these facts by showing him as a shabby, spectacled student who might have walked out of a play by Chekhov. This interpretation is ingenious and, as we have seen, it has some warrant from the text. It is not, however, entirely satisfactory. The royal guards, who were gentlemen, not the social equivalent of private soldiers of more modern armies, treat him with marked respect. At the end, he has a natural authority which enables him to take command of the corpse-strewn scene, and to speak with dignity, almost with equality, to Fortinbras who is in the full flush of his triumph over the Poles, and of the virtual certainty of succeeding to the throne of Denmark. A costume much like that of the other courtiers but less richly ornamented and perhaps a little shabby would convey the right impression. Other courtiers would wear variations of the costumes assigned to the major characters above.

One does not need to subscribe to the theory that Polonius was a satirical portrait of Lord Burghley to find Burghley's portraits full of useful information for Polonius's costume. Other portraits of Elizabethan worthies give additional detail; a dark furred robe over a dark but richly jewelled doublet and hose, a flat cap, perhaps jewelled also, and a chain and staff of office. His servant, Reynaldo, would wear his livery — ie, the same colours, striped — and boots to indicate he was about to go on a journey.

Nothing in the texts indicates the age of the Danish or of the English ambassadors. Availability

of actors may well be the decisive factor. Other things being equal, modifications of the Polonius costume would do well, with, of course, the addition of travelling cloaks and boots. The Gentlemen of the Guard would wear morions, breast-plate, long military cloaks and boots, and carry partisans. The grave-diggers or clowns would wear jerkins, hose and boots.

The nature and consequently the garb of the cleric at Ophelia's burial is a matter of dispute. Much of the play, especially the Ghost's references to purgatorial fires, implies a Catholic background. On the other hand, Dover Wilson emphasizes the Protestant implications of Wittenburg as Hamlet's university as well as Luther's. Adding to this the Second Quarto's speech heading of 'Doct.', he takes the priest to be a Protestant Doctor of Divinity, wearing a gown and tippet (black scarf) over a cassock and having a square cap on his head. However the producer may decide the question, Hamlet's reference to 'maimed rites', Laertes's repeated protests and the priest's harsh reply make it clear than anything in the way of elaborate ceremonial would be totally out of place.

Fortinbras's Captain (IV. 4) would wear much the same as the Gentlemen of the Guard, with perhaps a different coloured sash or shoulder-knot to distinguish Norwegian from Dane. Fortinbras himself should be in full armour to emphasize his function as the man of action, one of the many foils to Hamlet in the play. When the Pitoeffs produced *Hamlet*, Fortinbras entered the Danish court in magnificent white armour. According to all accounts, the theatrical impact was electrifying: here, one felt, after the corrupt luxury of the court and the tragic blackness of Hamlet, was the white deliverer, the Galahad who would restore health to the Waste Land of Denmark. It is rather doubtful whether this picture agrees with what we hear of Fortinbras, who 'Sharked up a list of lawless resolutes'. But the Fortinbras we actually see and hear shows dignity and sympathy as well as political opportunism. It is at least possible to present him, like Malcolm at the end of *Macbeth* and Richmond and the end of *Richard III*, as the 'Medicine of the sickly weal'.

For the scenes on the battlements (I. 1, 4 and 5), plate armour, of the sort still worn ceremonially at

The Travelling Players

The Player King and Queen

the time is not only appropriate to the style of this production, but also satisfies the references in the text. In Act I, scene 2, Horatio describes the Ghost as 'Armed at point exactly, cap-a-pe'. Later in the scene, this is confirmed by Marcellus and Barnardo. Horatio adds, 'he wore his beaver up'. For the Closet scene (III. 4) one may either accept Dover Wilson's recommended following of the Stage Direction from Q. 1 and dress the Ghost in night-gown, ie. a dressing gown, or may follow a tradition that goes back at least as far as Rowe's edition of Shakespeare (1709) and leave him in armour.

The Players remain. They must have two contrasting sets of clothes: their travelling clothes and the costumes for 'The Murder of Gonzago'. Their ordinary clothes should suggest a rather precarious, almost a ragged finery. They are down on their luck and would inevitably be travel-stained too. Boots, cloaks and broad-brimmed hats over brightly coloured but rather shabby, perhaps even patched, doublets and hose would give the right impression. For 'The Murder of Gonzago', their clothes should be impressive enough to make their appearance at court acceptable, yet tinselly enough to parallel the contrast between the verse of their play and that of *Hamlet*.

Apart from such Ladies-in-waiting as the company can provide and the producer considers helpful, we have only two women to consider. It usually succeeds best to portray Gertrude as a ripe autumnal beauty, with enough sexual attract-

iveness to make Claudius's passion for her convincing. And if it is not convincing, a whole area of the play becomes merely grotesque. However should we take the grave-digger's reference to Hamlet as thirty, it would be very dangerous to let it make Gertrude definitely middleaged. It would, of course, be quite workable to suggest that she was clinging rather desperately to the remains of her youth and beauty, but the efforts should be largely successful. Though the similar efforts of Shakespeare's own queen eventually failed, some of her portraits in early middle age are a useful guide. The portrait of her standing on a map of England, in the National Portrait Gallery, is one possible model. Here she wears a farthingale, stomacher, under and over sleeves and parted ruff, all of the same richly embroidered material. Gertrude's full-blown voluptuousness could be conveyed by a low décolleté and an overskirt open to show a totally contrasting underskirt.

Ophelia, before her mad scene, should also wear a farthingale and stomacher, richly though less richly ornamented, and her hair more simply dressed, though bound with pearls. For her mad scene, she could wear either her previous clothes torn and dishevelled or a plain white gown and bare feet.

Lighting

Skilful lighting can direct the audience's attention where it is desired. For example, the opening could show Francisco dimly silhouetted against a still dark sky. Gradual lightening could then give the audience an adequate view of the actors' faces and indicate the coming of dawn. Spots could follow Hamlet and the Ghost in I. 4 and 5. The Ghost's spot should have a distinctive colour to differentiate him from the living. For what we may call Polonius's domestic scenes — with Laertes, Ophelia and Reynaldo — light could be concentrated on a consistently restricted area downstage, leaving the rest in darkness. A similar device, but now using the whole of the downstage acting area, would suit the various corridor scenes. The whole stage and the full power of the available lighting would be appropriate to the first Court scene (I. 2), the performance of 'The Murder of Gonzago', and to the last scene.

Furniture and props

Most of these have been mentioned already or are sufficiently clear from the text. Some, however, need special comment. The thrones should be exactly equal to agree with Claudius's description

of Gertrude as 'Th' imperial jointress to this warlike state'. 'Jointress' was a legal term meaning that she had a life-interest in the state.

In I.2, the King will need an impressive-looking document to contain the 'dilated articles' he gives to his ambassadors. They should have a proportionally impressive document to give Claudius on their return (II. 2).

For the court performance of 'The Murder of Gonzago', extra seats — chairs, benches, stools and cushions — will be needed for the audience. The Players may perform at ground level or they may use a rostrum or rostra. Some of the extra seats may be set before the scene begins or may be carried on by court servants and the Players during the earlier part of the scene, before the arrival of the main Court party. In the latter case, it will be vital to avoid distracting the audience from important words and actions. The bank of flowers should be obviously artifical, to mark it as part of the play within a play.

The last scene will use the full stage, which can be set much as for the play, but there should also be a table for the rapiers and daggers, about six of each. The table for the chalice and flagons must be near the throne, but not near enough for the King to prevent Gertrude from drinking the poisoned cup.

Special effects

These are numerous and important. As usual in plays of this period, music plays an essential part. Flourishes of trumpets are specifically referred to (I. 2, 4, II. 2, III. 2, V. 2). There should be easily recognizable differences between the trumpet sounds associated with Claudius, Fortinbras and the Players. Trumpets are often accompanied by drums, and these vary from the ceremonial pomp of the King 'Taking his rouse' and celebrating Hamlet's success in the duel, through the military assertiveness of Fortinbras's approach to the dead march at the end.

Other special sound effects include the cock-crow (I. 1), the build-up of menacing crowd noises and the crash of breaking doors (IV. 5).

The Ghost's disappearance (I. 5) calls for special visual effect. One can of course simply allow the Ghost to fade into the background or the wings. This is often done successfully, but the later sounds of his voice from 'the cellarage' and Hamlet's repeated references to it, do make a downward exit more appropriate. To achieve this, one may use the trap in one of two ways. It may openly show steps leading downwards as if to dungeons or other cellars. This is both effective and comparatively simple. The second way is to keep the trap in darkness and project a dry ice mist from it, so that the Ghost simultaneously steps down the stairs and into the mist.

105

A History with a symbolic setting and stylized costumes

Richard III

There is strong evidence that *Richard III* ranked with *Hamlet* and *Romeo and Juliet* as outstandingly popular with Shakespeare's own public. The part of Richard has always been an actor's favourite. Burbage, Shakespeare's own leading man, made his name in it, as did Garrick in the eighteenth century. It was one of Kean's greatest successes. In recent times, Olivier excelled as Richard, both on stage and screen. Nevertheless, it is a mistake to regard *Richard III* as a one-man play. Skilful performers can make much of Buckingham, Hastings, Clarence and the dying King Edward. The four women are clearly differentiated, as, indeed are such minor characters as the three Citizens in Act II, scene 3. This said, it is also true that the producer will often get his best effects by thinking of the characters primarily as contributing to a stylized pattern.

This demands clear and confident verse-speaking to give full value to the play's enormous variety of rhetorical devices. These should not be slurred as though they were embarrassing weaknesses of the young Shakespeare. A company that is unhappy with them should not try *Richard III*. Yet in some ways it should be easier for us than for nineteenth and early twentieth century actors, who were so sheltered from the extremes of violence and treachery that they found it hard to take the Histories as more than melodrama. We should find the world of *Richard III* less remote.

Setting

'The Grand Staircase of History' is a phrase familiar to all who have read Professor Jan Kott's *Shakespeare our Contemporary*. In a vivid image, he expresses the basic theme of Shakespeare's Histories as a great staircase, thronged with ruthless power-seekers forcing their way up; with those in possession desperately hanging on, and with the failures thrust down to destruction. At any one moment, our attention is focused on the successful climber and his victims. As soon as he has succeeded, the irresistible hunter becomes the prey, and is finally hurled over the top of the staircase to join his victims in the abyss.

To translate this image into an actual set, we propose to use three levels, joined by two flights of steps.

Imagine a large, barn-like hall. At the acting end, the first steps lead from floor level to a platform stage only a little less wide than the hall. A pavilion is set at each side of this. A smaller staircase rises from this to a smaller platform, on which stands a throne surmounted by a golden sun, the badge of the King, Edward of York. Black hangings mask the space between ground level and the first platform; blue covers the back of this platform; crimson, the topmost platform. The audience is on tiered seats rising from the floor of the hall, and in galleries on the three sides not occupied by the acting area.

The different levels, platforms and steps symbolize the rise and fall of those struggling for power: Richard eliminating everyone who stands in his way.

Three questions immediately present themselves: sight-lines; distance from the audience; consistency in using the three levels.

The question of sight-lines can be solved in detail only on the spot, by examining the actual situation and directing the performers accordingly. However, the following suggestions may help. The lower stairs may be supported on narrow pillars to minimize obstruction, and several of the scenes on the lowest level are crowd scenes, where the general effect is what matters. Other solutions are to change the shape, size or construction of the stairs; or to substitute two smaller staircases, one at each end of the platform. This would weaken the symbolic impact, but it could be more manageable. One could compromise further by cutting the lowest level completely and relying on the throne-dominated upper staircase for the central effect.

The distance between actor and spectator is not a serious difficulty in a History, which does not demand such close contact as the more intimate plays.

The prime purpose of the different levels is to establish relations between the characters and to show Richard's inexorable progress from triumphant Wild Boar to dead hog. Once the relationships have been established, they need only to be reinforced by significant placings at crucial moments. For the rest of the play, movement may be as free as the producer's sense of theatre allows. This, incidentally, in the opinion of many who combine scholarly knowledge of Shakespeare's theatre with practical experience of our own, was probably the way his company used their Inner Stage. In the same flexible way, the different ranks may be associated with different levels.

The 'Sun of York' above the throne at the opening should disappear when King Edward IV dies, and be replaced by Richard's Boar when he becomes king, and finally by the Tudor Rose, of alternate red and white petals. This, the symbol of England's reunion after long and bitter division, should rise at the end, as a visual reinforcement to the new king's speech of peace and reconciliation.

In the first scene, we need to establish the throne as the motive and prize for the scheming and bloodshed; Richard as the man unscrupulously determined to gain it, and the others as largely puppets in his hands. Richard is primarily the actor's responsibility, but the sun-topped throne dominating the whole set should help by displaying the prize and fixing it in the audience's mind from the beginning. If the doomed Clarence enters on the Middle Stage and leaves down the steps to the Bottom Stage, while the 'New-deliver'd Hastings' follows the opposite course, the visual effect emphasizes the plot.

The Bottom Stage could be used for Clarence's cell in the Tower of London (I. 4) and for all street scenes. In III. 2, Lord Stanley's messenger could enter on the Bottom Stage, while Hastings answers from the Middle, perhaps using one of the pavilions as his house.

The Top Stage could be used for all royal entrances, and there could be theatrically effective variations to show how the three kings differed in their relations to the throne. The dying Edward IV should be carried on in a litter, be robed as he moves to the throne, crowned as he sits there, uncrowned and disrobed as he returns to his litter and is carried off to die. The uncrowned, and soon to be murdered, Edward V should enter beside the throne in Act III, scene 1, but never sit on it. In Act IV, scene 2, Richard's entry and ascent of the throne is clearly ceremonial.

On the night before Bosworth, the pavilions would represent the tents of the two commanders, pitched on the Middle Stage, equidistant from the throne. They need solid floors to which the furniture is fixed, so that they can be flown safely. Richard and Richmond would enter them while they still rested on the Middle Stage. When they are supposed to be sleeping, behind closed curtains, the tents would be flown to a level with the throne. This would emphasize both the separation of their dreams from waking life, and their rivalry. If safe and reliable flying is impracticable, the pavilions may be set from the start on a level with the throne, or they may remain on the Middle Stage. The former loses the separation of dream from reality but keeps the visual rivalry. It

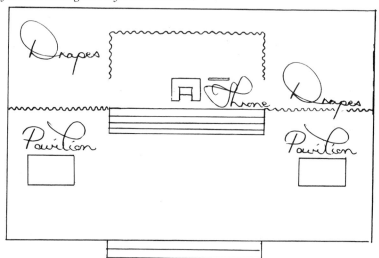

Drapes

Throne

Drapes

Pavilion

Pavilion

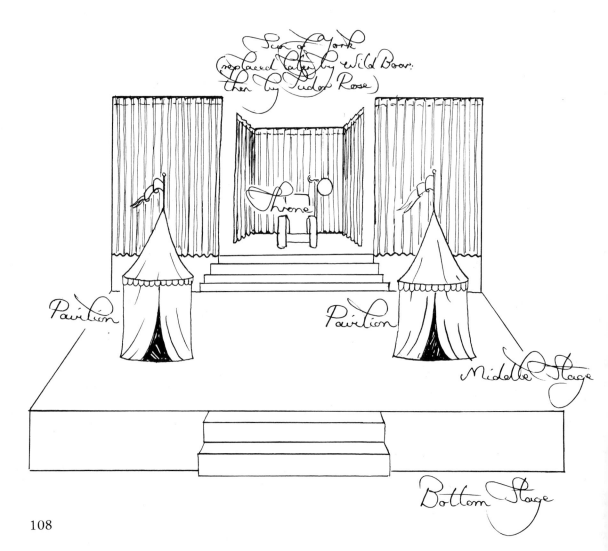

Sun of York
(replaced latterly by Wild Boar:
then by Tudor Rose)

Throne

Pavilion

Pavilion

Middle Stage

Bottom Stage

also demands a larger Top Stage. Keeping the tents on the Middle Stage avoids this but is less symbolically effective.

When Richmond finally defeats Richard in single combat (V. 1), he could drive him up the stairs and over the top. (There must be a mattress or some substitute to break Richard's fall.) At the end, the replacing of Richard's Boar badge by the Tudor Rose could be done in at least two ways. Either Richard or Richmond could dislodge the Boar badge in the fight — Richard grasping at it despairingly or Richmond striking it down triumphantly — or it could be changed by the stage staff.

Scenes that do not specially call for Top or Bottom Stage could be on the Middle Stage, with full use of connecting stairs for ceremonial and symbolic effects. In some scenes, such as the final battle, the whole set could be in use at once.

Costume

A production like this leaves the choice of costume open. It can combine with historically accurate late fifteenth century dress or with a simpler and equally effective base of black tights and polo-necked sweaters, worn below appropriately coloured and shaped garments with armour suggested rather than fully presented when necessary. The citizens could wear similarly shaped but differently coloured basic clothing, with cloaks, jerkins and hats.

The nobles can be further distinguished by richer headgear, cloaks, gloves, swords and sword-belts and jewellery. The out-and-out Yorkists can wear white; Lancastrians, red; the wavering and changeable can wear mixed colours, stripes and reversible cloaks. Variety of colour, length and shape can show personal differences. In several scenes, a change from short cloaks to long can emphasize the official and ceremonial nature of the action.

Gentry below the peerage, such as Ratcliff and Catesby, would wear similar but plainer clothing. These two, like Richard's other henchmen, might wear a smaller Boar's Head badge on their cloaks. As Lieutenant of the Tower, Brackenbury could have a stylized portcullis on his shoulder or his chest.

The three Citizens of Act II, scene 3 to be men of substance. Long cloaks in sober colours — grey, brown, dark green — would suggest their status.

Guards, sentries and other ordinary soldiers can wear knee-boots, long, dark cloaks, and perhaps morion-type helmets, and carry spears or halberds.

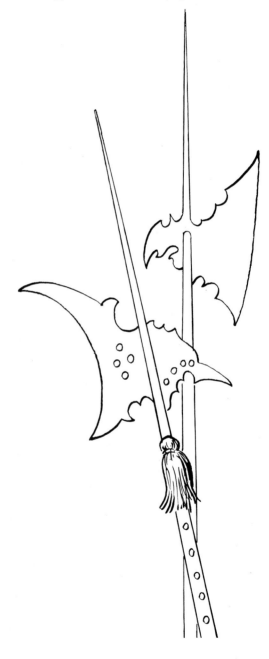

Civilians of equivalent rank would be much the same, minus the weapons and armour, but plus a variety of cloaks and jerkins, descending in quality and condition for the poorer members of the crowd in Act III, scene 7.

For the first three acts, Richard should wear a long, reversible cloak, black on one side, white on the other. The collar should be trimmed with ermine. The black side would have his personal badge, the Wild Boar, in white on the left shoulder. The white reverse would have the White Rose of York on a red background. The left shoulder of his sweater must be built up to indicate his deformity. He could wear a plain velvet cap. Belt and dagger are essential in all scenes: his habit of playing with his dagger is both well attested historically and dramatically helpful to the actor. It might be an effective visual irony to have him, the most lethal of all, the only noble who does not wear a sword until the battle scenes. The black side of his cloak seems best suited to those scenes where he shows his private character, such as I. 1 and 2, while the white is more appropriate to ceremonial scenes, such as II. 1. The distinction would sometimes be hard to justify logically, but there are differences of theatrical emphasis that such changes could underline. Plain black shoes with buckles would serve, except for Act III, scene 5 and for the latter part of the play, from IV. 4 on, when boots are necessary.

For Act III, scene 5, he could discard his cloak to show the battered armour referred to in the text. Act IV, scene 2 is virtually part of his coronation, so he should wear the same crown and royal robe as his predecessor. For this scene and the rest of the play, he could wear his George (a jewelled figure of St George killing the dragon) on his breast. The Garter he could wear all the time. For the march to Bosworth and on to the end, sword, helmet with crown encircling it and shield are sufficient emblems of war for this production. The shield would bear the royal arms of England. Over his armour, he might wear his royal robe or his original cloak, white side out, to show the Boar. This simplicity would have the additional advantage of making the disrobing before sleep and arming for battle as quick and easy as possible. It is always wise to avoid unnecessary chances for things to go wrong on the stage, and clothes have a diabolical habit of misbehaving at the worst moment.

Except for Act III, scene 5, when he must be in battered armour like Richard's, Buckingham should be magnificent in white and gold, suggesting a luxury-loving over-confidence.

The wavering element in 'false, fleeting, prejur'd Clarence' could be indicated by a pink lining to a cloak otherwise like Richard's white aspect. In the Tower scene (I. 4), he could wear a white night-gown or simply his tights and sweater.

Hastings, the eternal compromiser, could wear a pink cloak, indicating his attempts to placate both sides. A short cloak might suggest the dandified lover of Jane Shore. On his first appearance, he could be without belt and sword, to show he had just been released from prison. For III, 2, he would naturally wear a night-gown. In the Council scene (III. 4) he might exchange the short cloak for a long robe, more suited to his office as Lord Chamberlain.

The dying Edward IV could wear a white night-cap and gown when he is carried on. The business of robing and disrobing (see page 107) would express in theatrical terms that this was his last and failing act of royalty.

The two doomed princes should wear similar white tights and sweaters, and short cloaks badged with the White Rose on a red ground. Edward's kingship should be indicated by a diadem and perhaps a crown embroidered on the front of his sweater.

Richard III contains four named clergy of different ranks, who can easily be distinguished by simple insignia. Cardinal Bourchier should wear a scarlet robe and either a scarlet biretta or a wide-brimmed cardinal's hat. The latter is technically incorrect, as it is worn only at the ceremony when the new cardinal is created, but it would be permissible in our stylized production. The Archbishop should wear a simplified mitre and cope and carry a crozier. The costume of the Bishop of Ely and the two unnamed bishops who support Richard in Act III, scene 7 should be similar but less ornate. Christopher Urswick, the priest, should wear a black cassock and biretta. The scrivener would dress very similarly to the

Richard and Margaret

pirest, but would wear a plain cloak instead of a cassock, and have an ink-horn hanging at his belt. The Lord Mayor's rank can be indicated quite conventionally by a scarlet robe with furred tippet and a gold chain of office. The accompanying Aldermen would wear similar robes without the furred tippets, and with smaller chains or none.

Each of the four ladies must be considered separately. One pictures Margaret entirely in black, with a white face staring from the hood of the cloak she wears over her black tights and sweater. The aged Duchess of York would also to be mainly in black, but, though she has almost as much to mourn as Margaret, she is, temporarily at least, on the winning side, so her mourning would be modified. Her hood and cloak could be trimmed and lined with white. She could also wear some jewellery and perhaps some dull gold embroidery. Lady Anne, too, we first meet as a mourner, though a young and beautiful one. Her black, hooded cloak could be worn over tights and sweater of Lancastrian red; even her cloak could have the Red Rose on the shoulder. In Act IV, scene 1, she could wear the white Yorkist robe over her original Lancastrian tights and top, to symbolize her false position.

Like the other women in *Richard III*, Queen Elizabeth is doomed to sorrow, and she knows it. The contrast is that she begins in an apparently much better position: wife of the reigning, though dying, king; mother of the Heir Apparent. A gold robe over her white tights and top, and jewel-bedecked hair would project her rank on her first entrance. Her own performance, her words and the unconvincing consolations of her kinsmen, show the ironic contrast between appearance and reality. The same costume is right for Act II, scene 1. When she enters mourning Edward's death (II. 2) dishevelled hair could be a sufficient sign of grief: Shakespeare seems to have thought so. In her later scenes, she could join the other mourning women in wearing a black, hooded cloak. In her case, it could be worn over a pink top and tights, to suggest the temperament that made Richard call her — 'Relenting fool and shallow, changing woman': Clarence's daughter is a minute part, with little suggestion of personality. She could wear a featureless costume of white top over white tights.

Props

Most of these are too clear from the text to need much comment, especially as the stylized nature of this production frees the producer from worries about historical accuracy.

The coffin containing the saintly King Henry VI, should be open. The impression of Richard's hypnotic power over Anne is multiplied enormously if the wooing is carried on over the visible body of his victim.

Lighting

This style offers the most stimulating opportunities for imaginative lighting. Much will depend on the resources available. The practical minimum includes enough spots to focus powerfully parts of the acting area, so as temporarily to obliterate the rest; enough lights to cover the whole area effectively; and enough flexibility for all situations between these extremes.

One situation demands and another would benefit from special lighting. The first is the appearance of the ghosts of Richard's victims on the night before Bosworth. The ghosts of those we have seen alive in the play could appear as we last saw them. but in green or red light when they curse Richard, and in golden when they bless Richmond. The same lighting would naturally apply to Henry VI and his son. Henry should appear in his winding sheet, as we saw him in his coffin. The Lancastrian Prince Edward need wear only red tights and sweater.

The battle scenes *could* be played in straight, full lighting, showing all parts of the acting area, but a stronger effect might be gained by using stroboscopic lighting with red predominant. This would need care to avoid confusion beyond the dramatic necessities of battle scenes, but well handled it could make a powerful impact, and, by contrast, enhance the force of Richmond's closing speech. His promise of 'smooth-fac'd peace, With smiling plenty, and fair properous days!' could be visually reinforced by the change from blood-tinged chaos to a calm and steady glow of gold.

References

Shakespeare in the Theatre

1 LAWRENCE, W J, *Pre-Restoration Stage Studies*, 1927 p 162f and ADAMS, J C, *The Globe Playhouse*, 1943, pp 209-211. Both quoted by John Dover Wilson in New Cambridge edition of *Macbeth* reprint of 1951, p 146.

2 CHAMBERS, E K, *The Elizabethan Stage*, 4 vols, 1923, vol III, pp 77, 108 and 132. For special example, see comments on Juno's descent in *The Tempest*, New Cambridge edition, reprint of 1948, p 102, note 74.

3 CHAMBERS, E K, *The Elizabethan Stage*, vol IV, pp 131-138. Chambers, E K, *Notes on the History of the Revels Office under the Tudors*, 1906.
Cunningham P: 'Extracts from the Accounts of the Revels at Court, in the Reigns of Queen Elizabeth and King James, 1842.

4 JONSON, BEN 'To the Memory of my Beloved, the Author/Mr William Shakespeare:/ and What he Hath Left Us'. One of the poems prefaced to the First Folio edition, 1623.

5 HOTSON, Leslie, *The First Night of Twelfth Night*, London 1954, pp 99-103 and 106-112 for Knollys; chapter VI for reconstruction of original production.

6 JONSON, BEN, See note 4 above, and, for a more critical approach, 'Timber, or Discoveries' 1620-35. Relevent extracts printed in *English Critical Essays (Sixteenth, Seventeenth and Eighteenth Centuries)* Selected and edited by Edmund D. Jones, The World's Classics, OUP, reprint 1947, p 93.

7 DRYDEN, JOHN, 'An essay of dramatic poesy', 1668, reprinted in Jones: *English Critical Essays* (See note 6 above) pp 104-174, especially 148-152.

8 JOHNSON, SAMUEL, 'Johnson on Shakespeare.' Essays and Notes Selected and Set Forth with an Introduction by Walter Raleigh, OUP, reprint of 1957, especially pp 1-63.

9 SCHLEGEL, A W, typical example quoted by Hazlitt in his Preface to *Characters of Shakespeare's Plays*, Everyman Library, reprint of 1936, pp 172-174.

10 COLERIDGE, S T, *Essays and Lectures on Shakespeare, passim*, especially 'Shakespeare's judgment equal to his genius'; Everyman edition, reprint of 1930, pp 42-47. See also his reasons for denying Shakespeare's authorship of the Porter's 'low soliloquy' *Macbeth*, pp 163-64, same edition.

11 HAZLITT, WILLIAM, *Characters of Shakespeare's Plays', passim*. Preface gives attitude.

12 SHAW, G B, *Our Theatre in the Nineties, passim*, A good and easily accessible example is his review of Forbes Robertson's *Hamlet, op cit* vol III, reprinted in *Specimens of English Dramatic Criticism, XVII-XX Centuries* Selected and Introduced by A C Ward, World's Classics, reprint

of 1946, pp 208-217.

13 LAMB, CHARLES, 'On the Tragedies of Shakespeare (Considered with reference to their fitness of stage representation)', *Reflector*, 1811. Many reprints, including *Charles Lamb and Elia*, edited by J E Morpurgo, Penguin, 1948, pp 233-252.

14 HAZLITT, WILLIAM, *A View of the English Stage*, 1818, *passim*.

15 BRADLEY, A C, *Shakespearian Tragedy* 1904, St Martin's Library edition, Macmillan; reprint of 1958; *passim*. Good examples: treatment of Cordelia, pp 263-268; Hamlet, 86-102; some of the notes, eg B — 341; K — 368; CC — 413; EE — 419. See also L C Knight's essay 'How Many Children Had Lady Macbeth?' reprinted in L C Knight's *Explorations*, Penguin in association with Chatto and Windus, 1964.

Midsummer Night's Dream

1 BOWDLER, THOMAS, 'The/Family Shakspeare/in One Volume;/in which/nothing is added to the original text;/but those words and expressions are omitted which cannot/with propriety be read aloud in a family', 1818; 7th edition 1839, London Printed for Longman, Orme, Brown, Green & Longman.

2 CHESTERTON, G K *

3 HOTSON, L, *Shakespeare's Motley*, Rupert Hart-Davis, 1952, especially pp 82-85.

Comedy of Errors

1 ALEXANDER, PETER, *Shakespeare's Life and Art*, 1939; pp 68-69.

Twelfth Night

1 AUDEN, W H, 'Music in Shakespeare'; *Encounter* IX, 1957. Reprinted in *The Dyer's Hand*, 1962, p 520.

2 KOTT, JAN, *Shakespeare Our Contemporary*, translated Taborski, revised edition 1967, University Paperbacks, Methuen, p 229.

Macbeth

1 HOLINSHED, *Chronicles of England, Scotland and Ireland*, 1577; p 243, reproduced as frontispiece to New Cambridge edition of *Macbeth*, edited by John Dover Wilson, reprint of 1951.

2 Tracksuited production *

The Tempest

1 STRACHEY, LYTTON, *Books and Characters*, 1922, quoted on p 165 of the New Clarendon Edition of *The Tempest*, OUP, edited by J R Sutherland; reprint of 1962.

2 KOTT, JAN, 'Prospero's Staff' in *Shakespeare Our Contemporary*, Methuen, 1967 (revised edition), especially pp 238, 267-8 and 277-8.

Glossary

Apron: that part of the stage that projects towards the audience in front of the proscenium arch (qv).

Arcade: a row of arches on columns side by side. The arches may be open (as the set for *Romeo and Juliet*, qv); closed by doors and flats (as in the set for *The Comedy of Errors*, qv); or by curtains.

Backcloth: a flat painted canvas, at the back of the stage, hanging from the grid (qv).

Biretta: a square cap worn by Catholic clergy; black for priests; purple for bishops; red for cardinals.

Box set: an arrangements of flats (qv) to represent the back and side walls of a room; usually covered by a ceiling cloth.

Canions: the upper part of men's hose in the second half of the sixteenth century; they reached below the knee and were overlapped by the netherstocks (qv), which were often in contrasting colours.

Chiton: the tunic of ancient Greece.

Clerical bands: a pair of linen strips hanging from a clergyman's collar, before the Roman — or dog — collar became the normal clerical neckwear.

Cresset: an iron basket holding material being burned to give light; may rest on a tripod or hang from chains.

Cyclorama: essentially a smooth surface at the back of the stage, on which lights — and pictures — may be projected, to give a rich variety of effects. A full cyclorama is a solid curved wall; a partial cyclorama is shallower, or may even be a distempered back wall, which gives greater freedom for other scenery.

Doublet: a close-fitting, tight-waisted body garment worn by men from the fourteenth to the seventeenth centuries. It varied in richness of material and decoration; in its skirt, which was sometimes knee-length, sometimes a vestigial row of tabs at the waist, sometimes the in-between stage called a basque. The doublet was sometimes sleeved; sometimes sleeveless to show contrasting undersleeves. In the late sixteenth century, it was padded and boned; the most extreme form being the 'peascod belly' doublet, shaped to overhang the waist.

Farthingale: the characteristic ladies' skirt of the sixteenth and early seventeenth centures. A framework of hoops gave the required shape — bell-shaped for the Spanish farthingale, wheel--shaped for the French.

Flat: a frame covered with — usually — canvas on which the required scenery is painted. The standard flat is eighteen feet high; this is often varied to suit stage needs. Widths vary from one to eight feet, but for more than six feet, two or more flats are usually battened together. Flats may be solid or contain openings.

Flies: a space above the stage from which the

raising and lowering ie, 'flying' of scenery by ropes is controlled. Sometimes it refers to the whole space above the stage and out of sight of the audience.

Gaberdine: a cloak or long coat with wide sleeves, sometimes belted.

Grid: an open framework above the stage from which 'flown' scenery is hung.

Groundrow: a long, low piece of scenery, made of canvas stretched on wood; painted and with top cut to represent, for example, a low rock or hedge.

Halbert or **Halberd**: a long-handled weapon of the fifteenth and sixteenth centuries; its head had an axe on one side and a hook or pick on the other.

Jerkin: sometimes the same as doublet (qv) but also a looser jacket, often of coarser material. The latter meaning is used in this book.

Labels: strips of material worn over the tunic skirts of men in the Renaissance version of classical costume.

Morion: an open helmet, especially of the sixteenth century; usually with a curved brim.

Simple interchanging set comprising of flats including
2 archpiece flats
2 backing flats
Rostrum 23 cm (9 in.) high

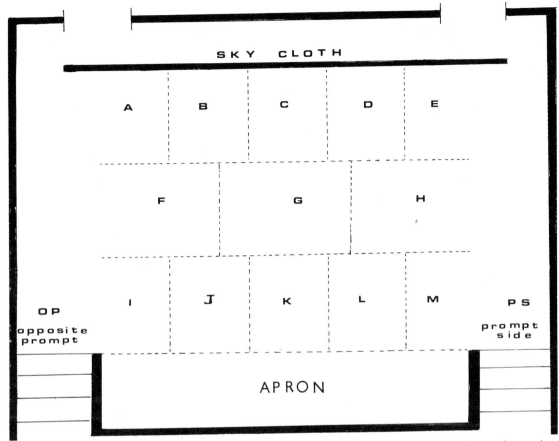

The stage is theoretically divided into area positions for all stage directions. It is essential to understand these positions especially when designing settings and stage lighting 'set-ups'.

A   Up Right (UR)
B   Up Centre Right (UCR)
C   Up Centre (UC)
D   Up Centre Left (UCL)
E   Up Left (UL)
F   Centre Right (CR)
G   Centre Stage (CS)
H   Centre Left (CL)

I   Down Right (DR)
J   Down Centre Right (DCR)
K   Down Centre (DC)
L   Down Centre Left (DCL)
M   Down Left (DL)
OP   Opposite Prompt corner
PS   Prompt Side (traditional working side)

Motley: (i) a material of mixed colour, usually grey and green. (ii) a long coat of this material became the common wear of children and natural fools. According to Dr Hotson, it was the garb of Shakespeare's fools, especially when played by Robert Armin.

Netherstocks: the lower part of men's hose in the sixteenth century, pulled up over the bottom of the canions (qv).

Periaktoi: a three-sided column, each side painted as part of a different scene. Being mounted on a central pivot, the columns can be turned to present each side as required.

Picadil: a stiffened and decorated border for the neck, shoulder or waist of the doublet.

Platform stage: the projecting main stage of the Elizabethan theatre, with the audience on three sides.

Proscenium arch: the arch that frames the main stage in most nineteenth and early twentieth century theatres.

Revolve: a circular part of the stage that can be turned by machinery below. A revolve that covers most of the acting area can be divided into segments, each with a scene set on it, enabling very quick changes.

Set: (i) noun: the collective name for all the pieces of scenery that make up one scene. (ii) verb: the act of placing scenery and furniture in position.

Slops: loose-fitting trunk hose or breeches of the later sixteenth and early seventeenth centuries; also the baggy breeches worn by sailors.

Stage-lifts: parts of the stage that can be moved mechanically above or below the general level of the stage floor.

Strike: to remove furniture and scenery.

Trunk hose: the common male garment from waist to thigh in the second half of the sixteenth century and the early years of the next. Trunk hose varied greatly in length and tightness. They were often slashed, ie cut into strips to reveal contrasting underhose, and the strips, called 'panes', were richly decorated.

Unities: these were Unity of Place, of Time, and of Action. Neo-classical critics, Renaissance and later, turned Aristotle's description of the theatrical usage of ancient Greece into rigid rules for all dramatists, insisting that the action of a play should occur in one locality (Unity of Place); should not last longer than twenty-four hours — preferably not longer than the time of representation (Unity of Time); and that there should not be any subplot (Unity of Action). They severely criticized Shakespeare for his disregard of these rules — though he did keep them in *The Comedy of Errors* and *The Tempest*.

Index

The letter (a) after the page number indicates the left-hand column; (b) the right-hand column.